George Barris (right front, wearing goggles) and his boys hard at work on an early customization job. George Barris collection

MY FIRST CAR

by Matt Stone

motorbooks

DEDICATION

Milt Stone and his 1934 Ford V-8

TO MY FIRST CAR GUY,

Milt Stone

1924–2009

First published in 2011 by MBI Publishing Company and Motorbooks, an imprint of
MBI Publishing Company, 400 First Avenue North, Suite 300, Minneapolis, MN 55401 USA

Motorbooks titles are also available at discounts in bulk quantity for industrial or sales-
promotional use. For details write to Special Sales Manager at MBI Publishing Company,
400 First Avenue North, Suite 300, Minneapolis, MN 55401 USA.

To find out more about our books, visit us online at www.motorbooks.com.

ISBN-13: 978-0-7603-3534-5

Editor: Peter Schletty (1989 Ford Tempo)
Design Manager: Brenda C. Canales (1969 Dodge Monaco)
Designed by: Cindy Samargia Laun (1980 Pontiac Sunbird)
Cover designed by: Todd Thyberg, Angel Bomb Design + Letterpress

Front cover: Peter Brock Collection

Printed in China

Excerpted from MY FIRST CAR by James
Lecesne and Marion Long, copyright ©
1993 by James Lecesne and Marion Long.
Used by permission of Crown Publishers, a
division of Random House, Inc.

    p.126 (Johnny Carson)
    p.140 (Dan Ackroyd)
    p.152 (Morgan Freeman)
    p.164 (Branford Marsalis)
    p. 200 (John Glenn)
    p. 202 (Tom Wolfe)
    p. 214 (Hugh Hefner)
    p. 222 (Andy Warhol)

Excerpted from *McQueen's Machines:
The Cars and Bikes of a Hollywood Icon*
    p.128 (Steve McQueen)

Excerpted from *Winning: The Racing Life
of Paul Newman*
    p.134 (Paul Newman)

As told to K.S. Wang
    p. 117 (Guy Fieri)
    p. 121 (Joe Mantegna)
    p. 145 (Gregg Allman)
    p. 154 (Mike Love)
    p. 178 (Ray "Boom Boom" Mancini)

As told to Tara Weingarten
    p.149 (Matt Scannell)
    p.158 (Neil Peart)

Young commander Glenn and guest appear to be swarmed by the early '60s version of the paparazzi. AP Photo/Ed Kolenovsky

CONTENTS

4 RUNNING ON ALL CYLINDERS
Athletes *172*

5 THE REST OF THE PACK
Journalists, Artists, and Others *192*

"Big Blue," Matt Stone's 1971 Oldsmobile 4-4-2

"My first car?
Oh, it was special, too.
At least to me."

INTRODUCTION

NO MATTER WHAT IT WAS, *everyone* remembers his or her first car. It may have been grand, or it may have been Grandma's. It may have been new, or beyond its last leg. Sparkling fresh from a dealer's showroom floor, or so riddled with rust you could watch it returning to the earth before your eyes. No matter what it was, love it or hate it, your personal Car Number One was *special*. At least to you. It is this notion—the acquisition of one's first freedom machine—that inspired this book.

The process was simple: identify a group of interesting people in the hopes that some combination of that person, the first car (or truck or bus or whatever) they ever owned, and its story would be interesting. I thought that, with luck, some of these vignettes would go beyond that: compelling. Eye-opening, even. Maybe a few would even be funny. I hope you will agree that the result is much more than that.

You'll read stories about rites of passage, family relationships, struggles and success, good times and bad, and many other aspects of life that remind us that the automobile is much more than mere transportation. As these stories were being related to me, most of their contributors reminisced not only about the machine itself, but also about the time and context in which they owned and drove it—the friends they toted around, a great (or not so great) first date, running out of gas, or the time(s) it wouldn't start. Many laughed. More than a few cried. My profound thanks to every one of them who made the effort to share their story with me, and thus, with you. Big thanks to Barbara Terry, K.S. Wang, and Tara Weingarten, professional writer friends who helped gather some of these great stories. As well as the many public relations representatives, personal assistants, secretaries, and managers who helped me pull all this together.

My first car? Oh, it was special, too. At least to me.

A young Gordon Murray with his first of two Hillman sedans. Gordon Murray Collection

I learned to drive in the mid-1970s, in between the two so-called "gas crunches" that occurred during that memorable, if in some ways strange, decade. Fuel costs had doubled from about 25 cents a gallon in 1972 to more than 50 cents a year later. America worried that fuel supplies would dry up altogether. The government stepped in with threats of mandatory gas rationing, and very real institution of the 55 mph highway speed limit. In spite of the scares, I thought this was the perfect time for a lead-footed, all-American, male teen to buy a 340-horsepower muscle car that got about 10 miles to the gallon.

My late father was a car guy of the first order. He loved to drive and loved hot cars of all stripe. He'd had souped-up Fords and several sports cars before I was born. The gene was passed along to me (although I obviously have a more mutant strain of it, because it let me to a life of writing about cars). Even before I got my driver's license (at 8:38 a.m. on my 16th birthday), I should have been thinking of something sensible and economical. After all, America had just witnessed its first gas shortage (or gas shortage hoax, depending upon how you view such things). All I could think about was something with a big V-8 engine and a four-on-the-floor. I looked at a number of muscle and pony cars before finding the sweetheart 1971 Oldsmobile 4-4-2 pictured on page 10.

"Big Blue" was on an Olds lot in Ontario, California, and had covered about 50,000 miles. It wasn't the super-fast, super-rare W-30 model, but had the standard, no slouch, 455-cubic-inch big-block V-8, a factory fiberglass ram air hood, a Rochester four-barrel carb that could flow more liquid that most toilets, and the requisite Hurst shifter. Power steering, power brakes, air, deluxe steering wheel, and an AM radio with two—count 'em two—speakers. Never a one-dimensional enthusiast, I liked cars that cornered well (for their size

and weight) and were fast in a straight line. My Viking Blue 4-4-2 did it all. To say I loved that car would be to define understatement.

After a while, I was lured into my first of several Porsches, and sold the Olds to my sister. She kept it as clean as I did and was the envy of every dude in her high school class, many of whom by then were confined to VWs and Honda Civics by the second gas crunch in 1979. I wish I could tell you I was smart enough to keep the 4-4-2 in the family, but I wasn't. I sold it, somehow knowing it was a mistake the instant we signed off the pink slip. If there's a noble aspect to this dumb move, it's that we sold it back to its original owner.

It was bought new in 1971 by a young couple in Chino, California. They drove it from their wedding to their honeymoon. The wife was driven to the hospital for the birth of her first two children in it. Family needs dictated that their beloved muscle machine be replaced by a station wagon. They sold "Blue" to an Air Force officer, who drove for a short while before being transferred and selling it to the Olds dealer from whom I bought it.

The couple's kids were growing, but they decided they wanted another special car. They were shopping for a Corvette when they saw the 4-4-2 sitting in front of my office with a "For Sale" sign in the window. She ran in the door, shaking and screaming, asking if the car outside was 603CKY—its original license plate. Trying to calm her, I said that it was, and asked how she knew that. She outlined the story above, and bought it on the spot for its full asking price. If I wasn't smart enough to keep it, I'm at least happy that the right people got to (re)enjoy it after me.

I hope you enjoy the ride, and that the stories contained herein conjure up a few memories about your first car.

—*Matt Stone*   13

1

At the Starting Line

RACERS

MARIO ANDRETTI
1957 Chevrolet Bel Air

"Who do you think you are? Mario Andretti?" That is a question uttered by countless police and highway patrol officers—to who knows how many speeders. That's because the real Mario Andretti defines speed. In fact, the term "been there, won that" defines him. He is an Indy 500, Daytona 500, Sebring 12-hour, and Daytona 24-hour race winner. Andretti has captured the USAC/CART open wheel driving title four times and is second only to A. J. Foyt in open wheel champ car race wins. Andretti is one of only two Americans to win the Formula One world driving title (1978). His career touched the corners of five decades, as he began racing professionally in the 1960s and competed at the 24 Hours of Le Mans in 2000. His sons, nephew, and eldest grandson are also pro racers. Although he's raced all manner of exotic machinery, he won his first race in one of America's most iconic cars: a Hudson Hornet.

The incomparable Mario Andretti at the wheel of a Ferrari 360 Spider, driving the Napa Valley backroads near his Andretti Winery. Author photo

"I grew up in Italy, where most cars were small and not very powerful. Big American cars were status symbols. When my family moved to Nazareth, Pennsylvania, from Italy not long after World War II, the idea of owning an American car, much less a new one, seemed like the impossible dream. But my dad worked hard and, ultimately, there came a time when we could buy our first-ever new car. We didn't know it at the time, but it would become one of the all time great American classics: a 1957 Chevy.

"My twin brother Aldo and I were teenagers at the time, already into hot cars and racing. So, naturally, we wanted to have some say in how the car was equipped. We went with my dad to the Chevrolet dealer to help pick it out. It was everything an immigrant kid living in Pennsylvania could have hoped for: a Bel Air hardtop in bright red, with a white top and that important 'Golden Vee' on the hood.

"Naturally, we had to have one with the V-8 engine. Ours was the 283-cubic-inch version with the Power Pack option. I think that raised the horsepower from 185 to around 220, thanks to the addition of a four-barrel carburetor, a hotter camshaft, and dual exhaust pipes. Funny, I remember telling my old man that the louder pipes helped save gas.

"Ours was particularly quick. We didn't do much to hop it up because, to tell you the truth, we couldn't afford it. A few other kids had similar cars and I drove a couple of them, but ours was just sharper, faster than the others. We all did the usual things with our cars back then: hung out at burger joints, chased girls, raced each other. Our biggest adversary, in terms of the street racing, that used to occupy so much of our time back then was a guy nicknamed 'Knaussie.' He spent a fortune on his car—a hotter cam, dual quad carbs, that kind of thing. But he could never beat our single-carb 283 with its factory Duntov cam. Years later, I met Zora Arkus-Duntov, the father of the Corvette, and we developed a friendship."

Andretti doesn't recall how long the car stayed in the family or for how much it was ultimately sold. His post-teen focus turned to racing, so street cars were of less consequence to him. Mario's first race car, by the way, was a home-built stripped-down 1948 Hudson Hornet that he and brother Aldo worked on and raced together. The boys were technically too young to compete at the local oval track.

The Andretti brothers' 1957 Bel Air, next to the family Buick. Nazareth, Pennsylvania, 1958. Photo courtesy Mario Andretti collection

When Aldo crashed it, nearly killing himself, Andretti says "my dad gave us what for." But that's another story.

Along with the original two-seat Ford Thunderbirds of 1955–1957, the "Tri-Year" Chevrolets of the same three model years are among the most popular cars of the 1950s. They were handsome, relatively light, straightforward, and offered solid performance. Although Ford outsold Chevrolet in 1957, the 1957 Chevy is arguably the most popular among the 1955–1957 models. Perhaps it was the car's big bold face or those crisp, pointy rear fender fins—and lots of racing success in the relatively new sport of NASCAR stock car racing— that made the 1957 Chevy the one to have. The availability of factory fuel injection, plus the performance and popularity of the full-sized Chevy's sports car brother—the Corvette—didn't hurt either.

One of the world's treasures of motorsport, Andretti succinctly summarizes his red Bel Air: "I've owned a lot of great cars since then: Ferraris, Lamborghinis, Corvettes, you name it. But my fondest memories are of that red '57. It's fair to say it was the only car I was really in love with. What I wouldn't give to have it back." ∎

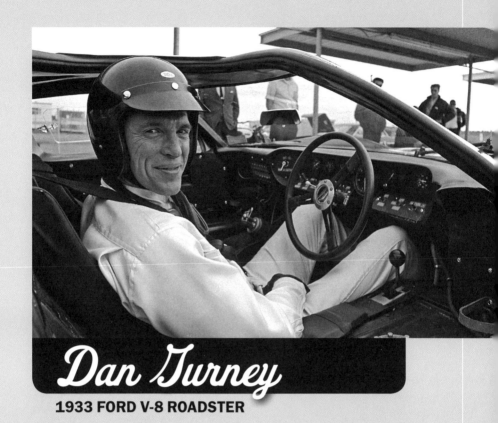

Dan Gurney

1933 FORD V-8 ROADSTER

Dan Gurney is one of America's great motorsport treasures. Gurney raced professionally in sports cars, Indy cars, Formula One (having constructed many of his own F1 machines) and won the 24 Hours of Le Mans teamed with A. J. Foyt in a Ford Mark IV in 1967. Gurney has won the Indianapolis 500 several times as a car builder and team owner, and won five NASCAR races in his long, illustrious driving career. Gurney's So-Cal-built Eagle Toyotas also won back-to-back IMSA GTP championships during the heyday of that series. Gurney's All-American Racers now builds a line of motorcycles called Alligators. His son Alex is a two-time Rolex Grand-Am series champion and a current competitor in the Grand-Am racing series.

Dan Gurney at the wheel of one of his faster rides, a Ford GT40, likely at Le Mans in the mid-1960s. Ford

"It was one of my first lessons in car control. Or lack of it!"

"My first car was a 1933 Ford Roadster V-8. I bought it for $325 from my friend in 1947. [He] was going into the Marine Corps.

"I did my first sliding in the dirt with it. I threw it sideways and stomped on the gas, but I was going too fast and the car kept on going in the same direction as I flew by the turn, missing it completely. I was lucky that it didn't hit anything. It was one of my first lessons in car control. Or lack of it!

"The next thing I did was send away to California for a Thickston dual carburetor manifold and linkage. It made more noise out of the carbs, but it didn't go any faster.

"That was also one of the many challenges that introduced me to the study of the internal combustion engines. My friend Dick Jarvis and I decided to rebuild the engine in a gravel parking lot behind the Strathmore Vanderbilt golf club. We covered the disassembled engine in blankets while we did the work. A milk truck backed over the crankshaft, but we reassembled it anyway. It was so tight that the starter wouldn't turn it over. Finally, after towing it around the block two times, we got it started.

"I liked most everything about it, except for the fact that the steering was very heavy and required a lot of effort. I ultimately traded it for a '40 Ford Tudor standard." ∎

Gurney cradling the bottle of champagne he sprayed the crowd with after winning the 1967 24 Hours of Le Mans with A. J. Foyt in a factory Ford Mk IV. Ford

DANICA PATRICK
1996 Ford SVT Mustang Cobra

Danica Patrick is one of the most popular drivers in motorsport. She was the first woman to win a professional open wheel series race, and recently launched her NASCAR career, where she is consistently competitive and a fan favorite. She was Indy 500 Rookie of the Year in 2005, and counts a Lamborghini Gallardo among her everyday drivers.

"My mother had a BMW 5 Series at the time of my 16th birthday, and that was going to be my hand-me-down first car. I was just at the point in my young racing career when I was going to make the jump from karts to cars, and the BMW had an automatic transmission. My dad didn't think it would be a good idea, and that it would be better if I had a car with a manual trans so I could get used to shifting, be able to work on downshifting, and such.

"I don't remember how exactly we decided on a Mustang Cobra; I think we all just kind of liked them, and you could only get them with a stick. This was before everybody had them. They were still kind of exclusive at that point. We wanted something with good performance too, because my dad had this theory that I was going to put myself in compromising positions by trying to pass people and semis and whatever. We lived in rural Illinois, and the farm roads were narrow. He felt that if I had horsepower, it would get me out of more trouble than it would get me into. The Mustang had 305 horsepower, 4.6-liter double overhead cam V-8, loud pipes, and a five-speed manual. We bought it new. It was a black coupe, and had a black interior, and was so cool. The SVT Mustangs were something a bit special then, with more power and better handling than the standard GTs.

"Within the first 8,000 miles, I went through two sets of brakes and went to racing-style brakes so they would be firmer and wouldn't wear out so fast. I put stiffer anti-roll bars on it, too. In the winter, that car was just a beast. I'd pull out of my driveway with my sister, on our way to high school. There was just a little gradual hill, and even just a little throttle with just the slightest bit of ice on the road, it would spin the tires and they just kept spinning. Sometimes it took a long time to get to school. Remember that it was my dad who wanted me to have a stick shift? Well, he drove it one time, and decided to try reverse while going forward, so it went in for a new gearbox. What was I going to do—be mad at the guy who bought me the car?

"Another funny story is that I didn't yet know how to do burnouts. People would ask me to do burnouts because it had a lot of power, and I would try to dump the clutch and hit the gas at the same time. I've since obviously learned, but I always thought it was funny that when I was 16, I didn't know how.

"It wasn't too long after I moved to England to race. The Mustang sat around for about six months or so, and when it looked like I wasn't coming home for a while, my folks sold it. I had some not-so-fancy cars for a few years after that—but this one was really cool." ∎

Danica Patrick swaps her IndyCar ride for a day of sports car testing with the editors of Motor Trend. Author photo

SIR STIRLING MOSS

1936 Morgan

Sir Stirling Moss is one of the world's most accomplished racing drivers. He raced successfully in Formula One, and also at the 24 Hours of Le Mans. He may be best known for his epic win in the 1955 Mille Miglia, at the wheel of the factory Mercedes-Benz 300 SLR Number 722. Moss remains a fully engaged enthusiast, is an honorary judge at the Pebble Beach Concours d'Elegance, and owns an OSCA powered by a rare desmodrodmic valvetrain-equipped powerplant. Moss and his wife Suzie live in London.

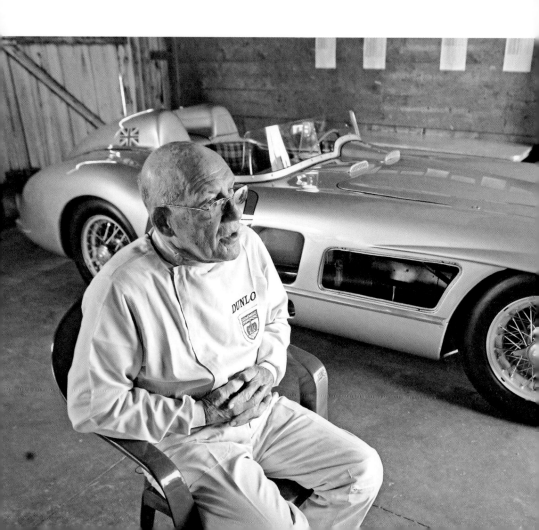

It's interesting that a man whose name was made on four wheels got his start on just three. Sir Stirling Moss collection

"The first car I had to drive on the road was a Morgan three-wheeler. It had a two-cylinder Matchless 1,000cc air-cooled engine. We paid 50 pounds for it, which was quite a lot in those days. It was considered a 'non-reversible tricycle' which, back then in England, you were allowed to drive when you were 16 years old. I actually drove illegally at 15, a bit prior to my birthday. It was quite exciting to me to be driving.

"One time, I had a problem with it when I was coming back from the country. I got a puncture in the [single] rear tire. The car swerved to the side, I went up an embankment, and the Morgan tipped over.

The Great Sir Stirling Moss takes a break and sits with one of his most famous rides, the Mercedes-Benz SLR, in which he won the Mille Miglia. Mercedes-Benz photo

It wasn't very bad; it just sort of gently rolled. My pet ferret was riding in a box mounted to the back, and I was very worried about it, but the box was undamaged and the animal was fine. It got a little oil on its head, but blinked at me and was otherwise okay. I managed to get the car rolled back over, and it was a pretty exciting event for me at a very young age.

"The Morgan was a lovely cream color, with a blue flash as I recall. It ran along really well, although I think it only had about 22 horsepower or something like that. It was a very rudimentary vehicle, but weighed very little. They raced them quite a lot back then.

"The great thing about having a car was that you could pick up the crumpet [girls] a lot easier than if you had a bicycle, of course. It was quite useful from that standpoint. Driving was quite fun back then as well, because there were far fewer cars on the road. I drove this car until I was 17 or so."

The Morgan "trike" cars were most unusual, with a motorcycle style V-twin engine (somewhat resembling that of a Harley-Davidson V-twin) mounted transversely at the front of the car. They had two wheels up front and a single in the rear, somewhat like a backward tricycle. This odd layout eventually gave way to more conventional four-wheeled designs with longitudinally mounted engines under a standard hood.

"Then my father got an MG/TD coupe, which was a very nice looking car but you couldn't see out of it very well. It was a very unusual car, and my father said 'Okay, you can drive this now.' It was frustrating, because after a while, he took the car away from me and I had to ride a bicycle. He then bought a BMW 328, in which he allowed me to drive in a couple sprint races in 1947. We didn't drive much on the road then, because World War II was only just over and there was petrol rationing and so forth. By that time, I was under contract racing an HWM [Hersham and Walton Motors]. I don't remember what happened to the Morgan, if we sold it or traded it or whatever." ■

Tony Stewart

1979 PLYMOUTH VOLARE

Tony Stewart is one of NASCAR's most popular drivers, racetrack owners, and racing team co-owners. A two-time Sprint Cup Series Champion, "Smoke" cut his racing teeth in various USAC open wheel series, ultimately winning the Indy Racing League championship in 1997, nearly winning the Indy 500 the previous year, his rookie season in the IRL. He is currently co-owner of NASCAR's Stewart-Haas Racing team. Stewart has been called a racer's racer, the type who will race "anything anywhere." He ran five Busch Series races for Joe Gibbs Racing in 1997. In 1996, he ran nine Busch Series races for Ranier/ Walsh Racing. He won an IRL championship in 1997, earned the 1996 IRL rookie of the year, and also Indianapolis 500 rookie of the year in 1996 after taking the pole and leading the first 44 laps. In 1995, he swept championships in USAC Midget, Sprint Car, and Silver Crown competition, and was the first driver to do so. He won the 1994 USAC Midget national championship, and he also won the 1991 USAC Sprint Car rookie of the year, the 1987 World Karting Association national title, and the 1983 International Karting Foundation Grand National title.

"My first car was a '79 Plymouth Volare. It was white with a blue vinyl top. Slant-six in it and it had worn-out front shocks so it bounced like a carnival 'hoopdy' ride car does.

"I was 17 or maybe 18 when I got it . . . probably 18. I paid $350 for it and it had been used as a mail route car out in the country by a friend of our family.

"I got my first speeding ticket in that car running 95 mph in Shelby County [Indiana]. That was as fast as it would go.

"Every two-hour trip to see my girlfriend used up one quart of oil. So I had to carry two quarts of oil with me—one for the outbound trip and one for the return trip. The good thing was, I don't think I ever washed it. It wasn't even worth the money to spend washing it. But it was a good car. It was safe and it was solid and it ran fine."

"I ultimately sold it. The scary part was that the guy who bought it lived in it for about eight months. That was kind of odd, I thought. I don't remember what I sold it for. It wasn't much. It may have been whatever I had in it." ■

Tony Stewart is often referred to a "Today's A. J. Foyt," so it's only appropriate that he runs car number 14—one of Foyt's old numbers—in NASCAR today. Photo courtesy Stewart-Haas Racing

Stewart is a multiple race team and racetrack owner, known as a guy who'll race just about anything anywhere anytime. Photo courtesy Stewart-Haas Racing

"I got my first speeding ticket in that car running 95 mph in Shelby County [Indiana]. That was as fast as it would go."

HELIO CASTRONEVES
1981 Toyota Cressida

Some people can do it all, and racing driver Helio Castroneves is one of them. The handsome, dynamic Brazilian has enjoyed a stellar driving career, and continues to be one of the most competitive drivers on the Indy Car circuit. He drives for veteran racer, race team owner, and mega car dealer Roger Penske. Castroneves' most significant on-track achievement to date is back-to-back Indianapolis 500 wins in 2001 and 2002. Helio showed the world another side of his personality, and another level of his physical talent as an athlete, competing on the hit reality television show Dancing with the Stars in 2007. Teamed with professional dancer/choreographer Julianne Hough, Castroneves won the competition outright, dazzling the judges, as well as American television audiences, with his ability and persona. Even though his daily rides include a Team Penske corporate jet and a 220-plus mph Dallara Honda open wheel racer, Castroneves' automotive beginnings were somewhat humble, in the form of an old Toyota sedan.

Castroneves celebrates his second of three Indy 500 wins.
Photo courtesy Indianapolis Motor Speedway

"My first car was a 1981 Toyota Cressida Deluxe. It was a champagne color, and had a beige leather interior."

The Cressida was the top of the line Toyota in those days, powered by a six-cylinder engine backed by an automatic transmission. It was a pretty vanilla machine, and was one of Toyota's early entries into the luxury sedan market (this was before you could get a six in a Camry, and a decade before the advent of the Lexus brand). "It was named Johnny 5," after the not entirely inanimate robot character in the movie, *Short Circuit*. Remember the line "Number Five is alive?"

Castroneves bought the humble Toyota in 1996, at the age of 21. He was born in Sao Paolo, Brazil, and began racing karts at the age of 14. He moved to America to pursue his racing career and bought the Cressida on a used car lot on Columbus, Ohio. "It was about 15 years old by then, and cost me $1,500."

What he liked most about this car were the same things that most Toyota owners value: reliability and longevity. "It never broke. It had about 170,000 miles on it, but I never had to do anything to it. Well, I did have to change the brakes, which I did myself—I'm very proud of that accomplishment! I also liked that it had air conditioning, and an equalizer for the stereo." Castroneves demonstrated his natural rhythm and an obvious passion for music on *Dancing with the Stars*, so a stereo system that allowed him to precisely adjust the tone control was one of the Cressida's best-liked features.

Downsides? Not many. "It made strange noises when I turned right. I hated that. I had to be a little careful—and was actually a little afraid—of making right turns."

Castroneves now lives in Coral Gables, Florida, and has a garage filled with the kinds of toys you'd expect of a professional racer. Helio currently owns a 2006 Acura RL, a 2004 Lamborghini Gallardo, a 2001 Oldsmobile Bravada sport/utility Pace Vehicle—among his gifts for winning the Indianapolis 500 that year—and a 50th Anniversary Special Edition Chevrolet Corvette, garnered for winning the 2002 Indy race.

What of the Cressida? It is no longer in the fleet. "I sold it for $300 to a young engineer. I then bought a Cannondale bicycle with the proceeds and took the bike to Brazil...where it was stolen."

Castroneves is a three-time Indy 500 winner, and one of the most popular drivers in the IRL racing series. ∎

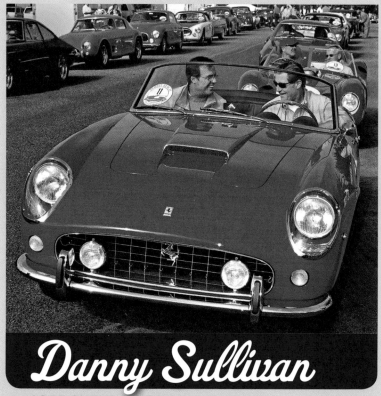

Danny Sullivan

1955 CHEVROLET PANEL WAGON

A native of Louisville, Kentucky, Danny Sullivan is one of America's most successful open wheel racing drivers. The one-time taxi driver competed in Formula One, won the Indy 500 in 1985, and was also a CART series national champion in 1988. He also raced in the Can-Am series, acted in several television shows, and worked as a television racing commentator.

"It was very cool. I was away at school in Florida, and I was not supposed to have a car on campus. I bought it from the original owner—a fisherman—in Venice, Florida, in about 1968. And believe it or not, the body was in really good shape and had no rust. It was only so-so mechanically, and it drank more than a little oil. I paid the guy $145 for it. After school, me and a couple buddies decided to drive it back to my home in Kentucky.

"By then, it used more oil than gas. I had it set up like my own little camper. I strung a hammock from the passenger side B-pillar to the back, and had a mattress underneath it so two of us could sleep in it. I was taking my buddy back to his home in Hamilton, Ohio, and the car sputtered and died. It just expired right there. So I sold it to a guy for $125.

"I saw it about a year later at a hot rod show and it had all been restored, and was spectacular. He wanted $10,000 for it. I had it only about six months—I lost $20 on it! After that, I bought a dark blue '41 Willys coupe. I've looked for another '55 panel wagon to replace my first and never been able to find another like it.

"It was dark green, and a pretty basic car with a straight-six engine; it was nobody's hot rod. We had such a good time in that old Chevy; just bombin' around with my buddies and girls and whatever, having a blast, being silly. We had no insurance—nothing. We were kids, we didn't think about any of that. Since we weren't allowed to have cars at school, I used to park it in the teacher's parking lot—talk about hiding things in plain sight. I remember I was dating a girl who lived a ways away, and it cost me more in oil than gas to get there. It ultimately became the bad boy's mascot at school. I'm still looking for another one."

Sullivan owns several great cars, and his collection won't be complete until he finds another Chevy panel, although he hopes for one that burns a little less oil than his first one. ∎

One of the great moments in Indy 500 history—and certainly in Danny Sullivan's career—was the famous spin-and-win tussle with Mario Andretti in 1985. Photo courtesy Indianapolis Motor Speedway

LYN ST. JAMES
1965 Pontiac Catalina 2+2 421

Lyn St. James was the second woman to qualify for and compete in the Indianapolis 500, for the first time in 1992, and ultimately raced in the 500 seven more times. She began racing in 1973 in the SCCA, and also competed in IMSA and the Trans-Am series. She has since hung up her helmet and has become a successful author and motivational speaker. Lyn is one of the strongest advocates for women in motorsports and established the Women in the Winner's Circle Foundation.

"*Never had an accident, plenty of speeding tickets, and there was a corner coming into town [Willoughby, Ohio] that we used to call dead man's curve and we'd play chicken to see who would let up first to make the corner, and I often won! I shouldn't be telling this story . . . hah!*"

"It was 1965 and I graduated from high school and had my first job as a secretary at the Cleveland District Sales Office of the U.S. Steel Corporation in downtown Cleveland. So I was definitely going to need a good car to drive. I lived about 30 miles east of Cleveland. My mom's car was a Pontiac Bonneville, so we were a 'Pontiac' household, plus a couple of my guy friends had GTOs (which I've dragged race a few times), so I headed down to the local Pontiac dealer to order a GTO. The salesman tried to convince me that I should buy a LeMans and not a GTO, but at the Detroit Auto Show at Cobo Hall I fell in love with the Pontiac Catalina 2+2 and put in my order: plum exterior, white interior, 421 motor, four-speed, heavy duty/high performance on all options. I think it cost around $3,500.

"I loved my car! Now, getting to work on time was sometimes a challenge, mostly due to traffic on the freeway. I found out that one of the guys in the office got onto the freeway at the same place I did and he drove a little sports car, I think it was a Triumph, so we often ended up meeting at the entrance ramp and saw who can maneuver through rush hour traffic and get to the office first: the British sports car or the American muscle car. So my penchant for racing really started early! And my love of high-horsepower cars also started early.

"Never had an accident, plenty of speeding tickets, and there was a corner coming into town (Willoughby, Ohio) that we used to call dead man's curve and we'd play chicken to see who would let up first to make the corner, and I often won! I shouldn't be telling this story . . . hah! Also, one of my guy friends was a musician and had a gig in Louisville, Kentucky, so we used to head down there on Friday nights after work and spend the weekend. I was the designated driver so everyone else could drink, and Ohio is known for cops handing out speeding tickets. We got stopped one time in a small town and the cop took us to the justice of the peace and he wanted like $300, which, of course, between all of us we didn't have. I was scared to death that I was going to have to spend the weekend in jail. This guy put us through the wringer and eventually let us go after we gave him all our money, which was about $100. The hardest part was trying not to speed after we left and continued south to Kentucky.

"I only had it [the car] a couple of years. I got married and my husband had a Porsche, so we sold both of our cars and used the money to put a down payment on a house. My next car was a Saab. Yuck! I wish I had that plum-colored, 1966 Pontiac Catalina 2+2 today!"

Although Lyn has retired from the cockpit, she still loves to drive, and continues pine for her big old Pontiac—anything fast with which to beat the boys. ■

My Darling
Rear Ended Again!
P.S. kisses!

St. James catches a ride with Trans-Am competitor Paul Newman.
Lyn St. James collection

> "My next car was a Saab.
> Yuck! I wish I had that
> plum-colored, 1966 Pontiac
> Catalina 2+2 today!"

Chad Knaus

1972 CHEVROLET CAMARO Z28 RALLY SPORT

Born in Rockford, Illinois, Chad Knaus grew up around the racetracks of the Midwest helping his father, John, race against big game stock car drivers like Mark Martin, Alan Kulwicki, Rusty Wallace, and Dick Trickle. By the time he was 14, Knaus served as crew chief during his father's Rockford Speedway championship season. The father-son combination also won the Great Northern Series championship and finished second in the NASCAR Winston Racing Series. A few years and seven track championships later, Knaus moved to North Carolina in 1991 to pursue a job in national stock car racing. Knaus is the first crew chief in NASCAR history to win four consecutive NASCAR championships with his current driver, Jimmie Johnson. He has also crewed for Darrell Waltrip and Jeff Gordon.

As told to Barbara Terry, excerpted from her book, How Athletes Roll

"I bought it beat up and junked, and worked on it, and tried to get it going."

"My first car that I ever owned was a 1972 Rally Sport Z28 Camaro [not the one in this photo], and that was a long, long time ago. It was cool. I bought it beat up and junked, and worked on it, and tried to get it going. But it all did not work out quite the way I wanted it to. And after that I had a Chevrolet Blazer, then a handful of other cars. I had a couple other Camaros, including a Camaro SS, and just some things like that.

"I currently drive a Chevrolet Tahoe, and I have a BMW M5, and a 2003 Porsche Carrera 4S, a Silverado pickup, and four motorcycles. I recently bought a second-generation Camaro Z28, just what my first car was, and I've always wanted to get another one. It's a great car to drive. I actually got it from [race team owner Rick] Hendrick. He started the Hendrick Performance Group. It is on-site here [near the NASCAR race shops], so we have a lot of very skilled race car mechanics and fabricators that are working on these cars. Rick located [the Camaro], and the guys here at Hendrick Motor Sports have done some engine and electronic work to it. So it has turned out to be an awesome ride.

"I also have a '66 Chevy Nova. My father built it when I was about 14, then he sold it, and the guy that bought it from my father approached me last year and asked if I wanted to buy it back." ∎

RYAN NEWMAN
1974 Triumph TR6

Popular NASCAR driver Ryan Newman hails from South Bend, Indiana, and competes for Stewart-Haas Racing in the NASCAR Sprint Cup Series. In 2000, Newman made his stock car debut in ARCA race at Michigan, then won the next race he entered at Pocono. He also won ARCA races that year at Kentucky and Charlotte. In 1999, he won the USAC Coors Light Silver Bullet Series national championship with two wins and 12 top-10 finishes. He won seven times in midgets and once in sprint cars, earned rookie of the year honors in Sprint Cars (1999), USAC Silver Crown (1996), and USAC National Midgets (1995). He was also the 1993 All-American Midget Series champion and rookie of the year. In 2008, Newman finished 17th in series points. He opened the 2008 season by winning the 50th Daytona 500, and had eight top-10 finishes and won one pole (Phoenix spring race).

"I'm king of the world!" A triumphant Newman climbs aboard his NASCAR Dodge to celebrate winning the Daytona 500 in 2008. Dodge

*Grampa's old TR6 is in good hands with NASCAR star Newman.
Courtesy Ryan Newman collection*

"It was a 1974 Triumph TR-6—yellow. I got it when I was 15; so around 1990. It was my grandfather's car, and he had a stroke. He couldn't drive the car anymore because it was a stick shift. My grandfather was going to sell it, but my dad convinced him to give it to me and let me use it for my first car. I still have it, and I still drive it today. It was a gift from my grandfather.

"I drove it to Pike's Peak from Indiana for a race with a friend of mine back in 1998. I think it was probably the first long trip that I had ever driven by myself. I had only used the car really to drive back and forth from home and college. I remember thinking that I had never realized how small that car was until I made that trip. It was definitely small! And the good thing was, I only got pulled over one time.

"I love it because it reminds me so much of my grandfather. I still have it, and I still drive it every once in a while. It's kind of cool because I still have his old sunglasses that he wore when he drove the car. When I get in the car and drive it, I wear the sunglasses. They're big Buddy Holly–looking sunglasses, but it's cool. I have no plans to part with it." ■

RACERS

2

Driving the Corporate Ladder

TITANS
OF THE
AUTO
INDUSTRY

GORDON MURRAY

1956 Hillman Minx

Gordon Murray has designed many championship winning Formula One race cars. The winter of 1969 saw a move to the United Kingdom to pursue racing car design. There followed a 17-year period with the Brabham Formula One team and an 18-year period at McLaren, both Formula One and Road Car Design. He is also the driving force behind the McLaren F1, which many still consider the ultimate exotic car of all-time. Today, Murray is head of his own design consultancy in England.

"I was born in South Africa, and grew up next to the sea. My father was a motor mechanic, and from about six years old, I was surrounded by a motor racing family. Nearly every weekend, we went to a motor race, and my father used to work on 'specials,' where people took road cars, made custom aluminum sports car bodies for them, and raced them around Durbin and Natal. So, I had racing and cars in my blood from a very young age.

"In South Africa, you had to be 18 before you could drive a car. But at 16, you could drive up to a 50cc motorcycle. That was before the era of Japanese bikes; all the motorcycles we had were Italian. They all looked the same: big tank, drop handlebars, single-cylinder 50cc two-stroke engine. Mine was a Maserati, a lovely little bike, which my dad bought as a non-runner, for 10 pounds. I rebuilt the engine and ran it for two years. It was always hot around Durbin, so we used to all ride in shorts and t-shirts. No gloves, no helmets, and I used to fall off at least once a month and lose acres of skin. It's a miracle I survived that lot until I turned 18, getting my driving license on my birthday.

"All I ever wanted to be was a racing car driver, not a designer. From six years old on, I never went through any other stage. My notebooks at school were full of sketches of racing cars. I was just car mad, and couldn't wait to get my hands on a car. We were working class South Africans, and my parents never had any money. My dad said, 'Look, I can afford about 150 quid [pounds] for a car, that's it.' I had my heart set on a '59 Austin-Healey Sprite—the frogeye one—which I thought was such as cool little car. This was 1964, so even the cheapest second-hand one was only five years old and still cost 300 pounds.

"My dad found a medium-to-high mileage, overhead-valve engined, '56 Hillman Minx four-door sedan. It had a light blue bottom and a gray roof. We paid about 160 quid for it. It was my sort-of 18th birthday present. It was far from sporting, about 1,340cc as I recall, and the car weighed far too much for the amount of power it made. It had a four-speed gear change on the steering column. Just not a very sporty machine at all. I got stuck right into it.

Gordon Murray has worked for Brabham and McLaren, but now heads his own independent design firm in England. Gordon Murray Design

TITANS OF THE AUTO INDUSTRY

A young Gordon Murray with his first of two Hillman sedans.
Gordon Murray Collection

"In those days, you took the hubcaps off and painted the wheels silver to make them sort of look like aluminum. I painted a racing stripe down the side, and got a racing mirror for it. I took tin snips and cut a hole in the floor, and bought a second-hand Sunbeam Rapier floor gearchange for the transmission, and chucked away the column gearshift. I think we also knocked a few holes in the muffler. Anything I could do to make it a bit more racy.

"I drove it like a lunatic. I only took four or five weeks before I completely wrote the car off, and nearly myself in the process. I was driving to a party with one of my mates. It was raining, and I was driving way too fast through a corner—appropriately enough named Cemetery Bend—when I lost it about 60 or 70 miles an hour. We hit a bus, doing about 50 miles an hour, coming the other way.

"The car folded itself in half around the front of the bus, skidding along the roof off the back off the bus before shooting across the road and demolishing a brick shop front. The Hillman was reduced to a little ball of steel. The roof had been crushed down below the back of the seat, and I was sticking halfway out the windscreen.

"I cracked my skull, broke ribs, my wrist, and injured my friend, fortunately not too seriously, who was in the car with me. Firemen from emergency services had to cut me out of the car.

"After I got out of the hospital, my dad said, 'Right, that's it. I'm not paying for any more cars.' I set about borrowing money from my aunt and various members of my family and bought another, identical car, which was black. It think it cost me about the same 160 quid. I went to the breaker's yard where my original Hillman was, and took all the modified parts off of it to apply to the new one.

"I've got such great memories of these cars. As noted, I was a lunatic driver, but I was pretty quick with it. The roads in Durbin flood very easily, because they got greasy from the diesel from all the buses and trucks. All my mates would phone me up to take them for rides at night. We didn't know it at the time, but we were drifting.

"Watch *American Graffiti*, and you'll see exactly my upbringing. Durbin, in those days, was interesting because we had all this Americana about, including milkshake bars. We had a thing back then for about four years (until someone got killed) called the Sunday Night Burns. Anybody who had a modified car used to collect at this milkshake bar right by the beach, and everyone would walk around looking at the cars. We'd look under the bonnets and you'd say what cam you were running, or double Webers, or whatever, and guys would pick races with each other.

After balling up his first Hillman, and recovering from his injuries, Murray found a near identical replacement. Gordon Murray Collection

"Now you buy a new GTI and it's already fast and has a lot of electronics in it. Back then, I couldn't afford anything fast like a Mini Cooper S or a Lotus Cortina [a race-bred Ford Cortina running a Lotus twin-cam four cylinder racing engine], and we all worked on our cars. I fashioned a big copper pipe that I stuck on to the end of my Hillman's exhaust, and used to run around the parking lot with my choke pulled out so it sounded like I had a tuned engine in it. It made such a nice burbly noise. About 11 o'clock, there would be some secret signal, a couple of car doors would slam, and the first two guys would take off. Then everybody would leave the parking lot, and drive about 40 miles to the North to a place near the North Coast where there was a two-mile stretch of straight road. Then, just like in America, somebody would stand in the middle of the road with a handkerchief, and there would be these street races with something like 300 cars parked up watching. The old Hillman went 40 miles up and down to those races nearly every Sunday night, although I didn't race.

"I'm always telling my son not do dangerous stuff. But I can't believe the stuff we used to do. I used to drive the car up those same roads, through the sugar cane fields, with three people in the back seat. Then we'd open the back windows, and the trick was to climb out of the window, across the roof, and down into the other side window, without anybody helping you, and the car doing 50 to 60 miles an hour. One guy would do it, and you'd shuffle along the seat until it was your turn. Stupid.

"I had an almighty wreck at in the second Hillman as well, at an intersection. It wasn't my fault, although I was going way too fast. The impact pushed the wing [fender] into the door so you couldn't open it. I panelbeat that one out myself with a hammer so I could drive it. I spun it off all the time, hitting trees and poles and such. After about a year, I sold it and bought a MK I Ford Cortina. I promptly took the engine apart, and tuned it up to 1,340cc. And then a Mini, which I also tuned. By then I was into designing and building my own race cars.

"My best memory of the Hillmans is those late night rides with my mates in the rain. I'd really mastered the art of four-wheel drifting, and the speeds were quite high. It was quite exciting. Things were just loony in those days. I wonder how we ever got away with it." ∎

CRAIG JACKSON
1966 Pontiac Le Mans

Craig Jackson is chairman of the Barrett-Jackson Auction Company, which produces collector car auctions around the country. He is the son of Russ Jackson, one of the company founders, and as you can imagine is a committed car enthusiast. Jackson owns many rare muscle cars and is also an avid motorcyclist. He still owns his first car, and plans on restoring it as a project with his children.

Craig Jackson is still an avid muscle and sports car collector, seen here with two of his Corvettes. *Photo courtesy Barrett-Jackson*

Jackson's first car, not long after receiving it as a gift from his grandmother. Craig Jackson Collection

"When I was 15-and-a-half and just about to get my learner's permit, my grandmother bought a new 1976 Nova and gave me her 10-year-old Le Mans. I spent that June and July, during the summer between my sophomore and junior years in high school, fixing it up. It had to be done so I could drive it myself on the day I got my driver's license in August when I turned 16. This photo was taken a few months later, on Christmas Day 1976.

"I grew up working on cars and dirt bikes. I apprenticed under my brother and spent my spare time at my dad's restoration shop. One of the guys there helped me paint the Pontiac, and we did it in a Cadillac Firemist blue metallic. I did all the stuff to it that we did back in those days, 'cause I sure didn't want it to look like a grandma's car, which, funny enough, was what it really was when I got it. I put chrome wheels on it with baby moon hubcaps, headers with a Thrush exhaust system coming out the side. I put a hot cam in it, and a stereo. That was the first round. As planned, on the day I turned 16, I took it out on a date to the drive-in.

"Later, I changed the trans from the old Powerglide to a three-speed Turbo 400 automatic, with a console and a Hurst 'his and hers' Dual-Gate shifter. I put a B&M shift kit in the trans, along with a high stall speed torque converter. I installed air shocks and jacked it up in the back. My brother thought that was totally obnoxious, which of course made it pretty cool to me.

"Even after all this, it wasn't all that fast, as I was still running the original 326, not a 389 like a GTO had. I was going through some stuff the other day and found one of my drag strip time slips, and it only ran 14s. It was all I had and it was all I could afford, but it was my first car. I cussed it out occasionally, because Pontiac engines with headers were a real pain, and it blew the header gaskets out all the time. It was a love-hate relationship, but mostly love. We used to cruise Central Avenue in Phoenix, to the State Fair, to the midnight drag races.

"After a year or so, and a lot hard running, the engine spun a rod bearing. I got a Corvette, which I restored from the ground up. But I kept the Pontiac with the intention of restoring and probably resto-modding it. I was going to have someone like Chip Foose or one of the other custom car builders do it, but I'm building a shop at my home and I think I'm going to do it myself. But do it right this time, and with my kids. Twenty years ago I saw a Ram Air IV short block and a 455 Super-Duty short block for sale and bought them. Plus I still have the original 326, so I've got plenty of engines for it. I'll build one of them up with modern ignition and fuel injection.

"Why didn't I just sell it? I don't know. With the engine blown and out of it, it wasn't really worth much. I had bought a GTO hood for it, and had always planned on turning it into a GTO clone [as the LeMans and the more performance oriented GTO were based on the same chassis/body architecture, it relatively straight forward to reconfigure a more garden variety LeMans to resemble Pontiac's top rung muscle car]. I guess, even back then, I was a little sentimental about it. I liked the body style, and I just liked the car. It always had a place in my heart. That's why I've dragged it around with me all these years, as many times as I've moved. And that includes all the parts I bought for it.

"Some may wonder why people like cars so much, and I think part of that is because, as a kid, it was your first real taste of freedom. You don't have to ask somebody to take you somewhere, or you don't have to pedal. You can go pick up a girl and don't have to have your parents in the car with you. It was great to pick your buddies up and go cruising or go on dates, and it was my first taste of freedom." ■

CARROLL SHELBY
1934 Dodge Sedan

Race driver, race team owner, chili recipe king, and legendary car builder Carroll Shelby needs little introduction here or anywhere else. Like most people, his first ride was a modest machine. Nothing at all like the fearsome, race-winning Shelby Cobras he gave birth to in the 1960s.

"The first car I really drove a lot was my family's '34 Dodge, when I was in Dallas, Texas. My father took me to get my driver's license right after my 14th birthday, which was in 1937. I was in the eighth or ninth grade. There wasn't any test or anything; all you had to be was 14, and you just went to the Department of Vehicles and got it. We went down first thing in the morning, because he worked at the post office and had to be at work at 4 o' clock. I said 'Dad, can I drive you to work? I'll pick you up tonight.' He said 'Okay, just be careful.' I dropped him off, and then immediately drove on East Pike in Dallas, and got caught doing 80 miles an hour.

Carroll Shelby at the wheel of the first Shelby Cobra. Ford

The same Shelby at the wheel of the Ford Cobra prototype, nearly 40 years later. Author photo

"I didn't get to drive again for six months. My dad grounded me. I remember the cop grabbing me by the ear and taking me to my house. He literally took me up to the front porch by my ear, and said to my mother 'Well, here he is, ma'am. We caught him doing 80 miles an hour. All he had on him was his driver's license.'

"Shortly after that, my father got rid of the Dodge and bought a '38 Willys, which I promptly rolled over. My poor father, what he put up with. The first car that I bought myself was my daddy's Ford Model A that he carried mail in central Texas with. We moved there about the time I turned 18. The Model A was a 1929 four-door sedan, it was black, and I paid him $75 for it. I drove it for a while like it was, and then bought something else and turned the Ford in to a hunting car. We cut the top off so we could shoot out of it and stuffed the tires with cotton rags like you'd use in a cotton gin. That way you didn't worry so much about flat tires in the outback.

"Bill Miller was a buddy from Dallas—we were raised together just two doors apart. He and I flew together out of Childress Air Force Base. I got transferred out and gave him the car. He later got shot down in a B-17 over Germany, but survived, and ultimately went to work for Howard Hughes. I don't know what happened to the car, but he probably got rid of it prior to going overseas.

"Other people are going to have better first car stories than me, although I've had a lot of interesting stuff over the years, and I still have a Model A. But that original one was just an old car I bought from my father." ∎

Dean Jeffries
1947 MERCURY CONVERTIBLE

Dean Jeffries is among history's most legendary car designers, customizers, builders, and custom painters. He created many memorable television and movie cars, including the Black Beauty (from The Green Hornet) and the Monkeemobile. His most notable hot rod creation is likely the far-out Mantaray. Jeffries painted, lettered, or pinstriped dozens of famous race cars over the years, and he also repainted the first Shelby Cobra prototype in between magazine road tests and photo shoots so people would think it was a different car featured in each story. Jeffries modified or customized vehicles for James Dean, Elvis Presley, four-time Indy winner A. J. Foyt, and several other Hollywood notables.

Jeffries' first car, a 1947 Merc convertible, before it was repainted and received the full Jeffries pinstriping-and-custom-paint treatment. Dean Jeffries collection

The Merc now white and custom painted. Dean considers some
additional pinstriping.... Dean Jeffries collection

"This was in the earily fifties sometime, judging by the hubcaps on the car—I remember stealing them in the middle of the night."

My dad had a mechanic's shop in Compton, Caliofrnia. His partner was a body and fender man, and I hung out there every day after school. The Merc came into the shop with the front end all smashed up. My dad bought it, and we decided to fix it up and that it would be my car. We repainted it this dark, dark green—I hated that color. This was in the earily fifties sometime, judging by the hubcaps on the car—I remember stealing them in the middle of the night. I had just taken my girlfriend home, and it was 2:00 or 3:00 in the morning. Well you know how it is in the middle of the night when everything is all quiet, so everything you do sounds three times as loud. But I got away with it. I don't remember what kind of car they were on, but I liked these caps and thought they'd look great on my Mercury. I Frenched the headlights and took off a bunch of chrome too, plus I added Appleton spotlights. My dad rebuilt the engine, but it was dead stock. I didn't have any money for any hot rod stuff to put on it. The old top was rotted out and finally blew off, so then we put a new top on it.

Every summer, I'd take it down to Laguna Beach, drop the top, and cruise for chicks. That was the greatest. Sometimes we'd go up to Big Bear Lake, but most of the time it was the beach. Some of the best times of my life. I had a Merc convertible full of buddies and girls, cruising along the coast in Laguna—how much better could it get? It was about that time that I began doing custom work and pinstriping. Of course, I started out on my own car because I had to be able to show my work to potential customers, so I painted it white and striped anything I could put a brush on: my car, my toolbox, my refrigerator, a door in the house, whatever.

I don't remember how long I had it, four or five years maybe, and then I sold it to a guy from Akron, Ohio. I don't remember for how much, or exactly why I moved on. ■

"Some of the best times of my life. I had a Merc convertible full of buddies and girls, cruising along the coast in Laguna—how much better could it get?"

One of Jeffries' most famous creations, the Monkeemobile, poses with the 60s pop stars. Dean Jeffries collection

PIERO FERRARI

1963 Morris Mini

Being the son of Enzo Ferrari, you would think he could have any car he wanted, including one bearing his family name. But in as much as Ferrari the elder wanted his son to work his way up through the ranks of his company, it is also logical that he didn't feel it right that young Piero begin his driving career with one of his own V-12 powered creations. So he selected something a bit more modest. Piero Ferrari has worked at Ferrari since he was a teen and today holds the title of vice chairman. He is deeply involved in all of the company's activities, as well as in the development of each new model approved for production, and remains a committed automotive enthusiast.

> *"One day while I was driving along the roads running over the hills around Maranello, a Porsche drove up on me and obviously imagined it was going to overtake me easily. But in that case the Porsche found it hard to keep up."*

"My first car was a red, white-roofed Morris Mini 993 (with an upgraded 1,300cc engine), which I got in 1963. I don't know how much it cost. It was a present from my father who knew and admired Alec Issigonis, the man who designed that great car."

"My memories of those years included two, which were very much linked to the Mini. One day while I was driving along the roads running over the hills around Maranello, a Porsche drove up on me and obviously imagined it was going to overtake me easily. But in that case the Porsche found it hard to keep up. We stopped and the owner of the Porsche wanted a closer look at my Mini and decided there and then he was going to sell his Porsche and buy one. Then another day, this time in the evening, I was driving along the main road from Rimini and I saw some headlights gaining on me and didn't know who it could be. I thought that I'd manage to outrun whoever it was the same way as I did with the Porsche, but instead the car just shot past me. And as it went by I realised it was a Ferrari, and thought, well, that's okay I suppose!

As time goes along, Piero Ferrari more closely resemble his famous father, and company founder, Enzo Ferrari. Ferrari

Bottom: Piero Ferrari drives the Mini that was restored and
given to him as a gift. Top: Enzo Ferrari had great respect for
the Mini's innovative packaging, use of space, and engineering.
Photos courtesy Piero Ferrari collection

"What I most liked about the Mini was its road holding, which was great and really gave you wonderful driving performance. As for any defects, there was only one, though I can hardly say it was much more than an annoyance. When I turned off the windscreen wipers they wouldn't go back to their rest position automatically, so I had to wait the right time and turn the wipers back on. I managed to develop quite a skill and sense of timing with those wipers.

"I sold the car on to a friend of mine a few years later, though I can't remember the price. Then he had an accident in it and sold it again and I lost track of it. Fortunately some very dear friends of mine who knew what that car meant to me gave me an identical Morris Mini for my 60th birthday, an original model which had been restored, red with a white roof, which I still enjoy driving, especially in summer, over the hills around Maranello." ■

"Fortunately some very dear friends of mine who knew what that car meant to me gave me an identical Morris Mini for my 60th birthday, an original model which had been restored, red with a white roof, which I still enjoy driving, especially in summer, over the hills around Maranello."

GLENN MOUNGER
1947 Ford Super Deluxe Station Wagon

Not many of us had the vision to hang on to our first car. In some cases, the car no longer exists, through accidents, lack of maintenance, or a variety of reasons. Most likely it wasn't deemed worth hanging onto at the time. But any of these circumstances may not have eradicated the owner's passion for it. A suitable facsimile is often located or built, and it's usually enough to evoke those good old memories. Glenn Mounger's collection is extensive and eclectic, and his reputation as an automotive expert, collector, and enthusiast is known worldwide. After two successful ventures in the clothing business, Mounger retired and assumed the helm of the world's most significant car show, the Pebble Beach Concours d'Elegance. Mounger has since given up that post, but remains involved as chief honorary judge.

"Reminiscing about my first car invokes memories of fun and freedom. My first car purchase was influenced by family vacations to Hawaii where I had envisioned myself someday becoming a surfer. However, I lived in Seattle. And while there was no sand or surf, there are a lot of great hills. It was 1961 and my buddies and I had cut up old water skis and attached rollerskate wheels and thus started "sidewalk surfing." Groups like Jan and Dean and the Beach Boys were starting to become popular, and we all dreamed of moving to California or Hawaii to become real surfers. And a real surfer has to have transportation.

"For years I had noticed the car. Every time we drove down Thorndyke Avenue I looked and expected it to be gone. How could someone leave such a cool car just sitting there? It *was* the ultimate surfer's car—a 1947 Ford Super Deluxe Station Wagon Woody! Considered by many to be the ultimate surfer wagon, which makes sense, as during the postwar birth of the surfing phenomenon, these cars were plentiful, cheap, with a long flat roof to which longboards could be easily attached, and enough room in back to sleep or live in. This wagon was painted Glade Green with brown interior, and all three bench seats were intact, as well as its metal spare tire cover.

The wood had suffered from years of neglect and the inside smelled of mold. The '47's tires were cracked and about half full of air, and the exhaust system was dragging on the ground. I had just turned 14 a few months earlier, and of course, none of the above mattered to me one bit. I was going to buy that car.

"I brought my buddy Boe Fletcher with me for moral support and we made the long walk over to the house where the Ford was parked. I brought all the money I had—$15—but was concerned that it might not be enough to buy it, so Boe told me that he had $5 at home and, if necessary, I could offer that to sweeten the deal. As we walked up to the owner's door and rang the bell I noticed that Boe was a comfortable 30 feet behind me saying, 'Go ahead, Mounger. You can do it.'

"After a seemingly interminable wait, the biggest man I have ever seen, and covered with hair, opened the door, peered down at

Mounger with the modern day version of his first car. This one, however, has none of the rust or wood rot that brought down his first one. Richard Culp

> # "And a real surfer has to have transportation."

me and said, 'Yeah? What do you want?' Without hesitation, I told him I wanted to buy his old station wagon. When he asked how much I was willing to pay, I told him $15, but I might be able to get more if necessary. He asked if I had the money on me, and I said yes, whereupon he turned and went to get the title. My first major sales transaction!

"The word spread fast around my neighborhood that Mounger bought 'The Woody.' It was the coolest day of my life, at least up until that point. One of my friends had an older brother who had a license, and we proceeded to tow the Woody to a garage up the street which I had rented with Boe's $5. Over the next month we began the 'restoration process.' Unfortunately, our skill level had reduced the Woody to a pile of dry rotten wood scattered throughout the garage. In spite of how much I wanted the car, I realized it was beyond saving. Taking advantage of my new found sales skills, I was 'talked out of' owning the Woody by two classmates and cheerfully pocketed their $30.

"For years I was haunted by the memory of that Woody and what might have been. In 1978 I attended an auction in the Seattle area, and a wonderful 1947 Ford Woody with the exact same Glade Green paint was up for bidding. I had to own it but this time it cost me $15 plus a few zeroes added to the total [$15,000].

"We still own that old Woody and have enjoyed it for the last 30 years. Other than a few details, such as a Mercury crankshaft spinning in the old Ford flathead V-8 block, a set of burbling dual exhausts, and some period decals in the windows, it's restored to original condition. I drive it all the time, and especially enjoy taking it to the ferry dock to pick up friends. I'm finally living the surfer dream!"

Mounger freely admits that his original Woody was probably too far gone to restore at the time, and the magnitude of the project was far beyond his budget and mechanical ability. But you can't blame a kid for trying. ■

ED WELBURN

1965 Buick Skylark Gran Sport

Ed Welburn is vice president of Global Design at General Motors. Welburn grew up in an auto enthusiast family in the Philadelphia area. At age 11, he wrote to General Motors asking about a job as a car designer. The company replied with helpful suggestions and information about the GM's design internship program. He studied fine art in college, and ultimately earned a spot as a GM design intern. He was later hired by GM, and began his career there at Buick, and acknowledges his 1963–67 Chevrolet Corvette as one of his favorite cars and automotive designs.

"You would the think answering the question of 'my first car' would be an easy one, but in my case, it's complicated. Between the time just prior to getting my driver's license, and the time I went to college, I had four cars. I was always into cars, partially because I grew up

in Berwyn, Pennsylvania. That's were drag racer Bill 'Grumpy' Jenkins was from, and not too far away was Roger Penske's first car dealership. The funny part about all this is that I never actually drove what was technically my first one.

Ed Welburn is only the fifth individual to hold the position of design VP at General Motors, and the first African-American to do so. General Motors

Hey check out that hair! A young Welburn stylin' with his Gran Sport.
Ed Welburn collection

"My father owned an auto body repair shop, and as you can imagine, all kinds of interesting cars went through there. Before I even turned 16, my father bought for me a '56 Chevy. We worked on it and repainted it a really nice deep green. Right after I got my license, I had major knee surgery due to a sports injury. It was clear I wasn't going to be able to drive the Chevy for quite a while because it had a manual transmission—with a Hurst shifter—and a clutch of course. I never drove it! My dad drove it and enjoyed driving it, and then he sold it and got me a Corvair Monza.

"The Monza was an automatic, and it was a great car for me to get around in after surgery. I had a blast driving this car, and had it for about two years. It was a lot of fun to drive. Then I briefly had an Opel Kadett Rally, and then I got my '65 Buick Gran Sport when I started college. That's the one I consider my 'real' first car, and the one I have such a strong emotional connection with. I took it to college, and the trunk was the perfect size for all my art supplies, and my stereo, of course; one of the most important things when you're growing up.

"I ran through so many sets of rear tires, just lighting them all the time. The '65 Skylark body style was a fairly light car, and the 401-cubic-inch 'nailhead' V-8 had so much torque. Mine had the single four-barrel carburetor engine with an automatic transmission. At the same time, my father bought a '65 Buick Riviera Gran Sport with the dual-quad carb setup. We bought them both used, and there's an interesting story about them. If you look at the Buick brochure

The Opel Kadett was also assigned to Ed as a daily driver for a while, but he considers the sporty Buick his real first car, and his absolute favorite among the wheels he drove in his younger day. Ed Welburn collection

from 1965, one of the pages shows a green Riviera Gran Sport parked next to a red Skylark Gran Sport with a black top. Someone from our town purchased those two exact cars, drove them, then traded them in, and we got them.

"Not everyone had cars at Howard University. Every Saturday night, I'd cruise by the dorm and pick up my girlfriend, and all of her girlfriends, and head out to the parties. Gas was 25 cents a gallon, and all I needed was a couple bucks worth of gas and we could go anywhere. It was also a good street racer because it was such a sleeper. I couldn't keep up with the Hemis, but I could handle the Road Runners with 383s because again my Skylark was so light and had good power.

"I kept the car all the way through college, and everyone knew me there because of this car. I don't remember what we paid for it, but owned it for about five years before selling it to buy a '71 Pontiac Firebird Formula 400. That was a good car too.

"I have an awful lot of passion for this car. Jay Leno's first new car was also a '65 Gran Sport, and he and I talk about them all the time. It was my favorite. Since I begun remembering this story for this book, I've started searching for one on the Internet. I mean, why not? I'm looking at a couple. I would keep it stock but I'd upgrade the brakes, shocks, some suspension upgrades. I'm going to get one."

Given his position and standing at GM, Welburn won't have much trouble getting a potential purchase worked on or restored. ∎

BOB LUTZ
1948 Volkswagen Beetle

Recently retired from General Motors, Bob Lutz's career in the auto-motive business spans more than five decades. Often referred to as the boardroom's ultimate car guy, he's held executive positions at Ford, BMW, Chrysler, and General Motors, and most recently as a GM vice chairman. He also served as a jet-attack aviator in the U.S. Marine Corps from 1954 to 1965 and attained the rank of captain, and drove the pace car to start the Indianapolis 500 in 1996 at the wheel of a Dodge Viper, a car he is credited with helping develop and bring to market. Also an avid motorcyclist, Lutz was born on February 12, 1932, in Zurich, Switzerland.

"It was so basic. It had the 'pretzel-style' rear window, non-synchro four-speed gearbox, 25 horsepower, and one—*one*—instrument, the speedometer. This was the base model. I don't think it even had a fuel gauge. You used to have to flip a little lever for the fuel reserve if you ran out. The seat fabric looked like industrial burlap of some sort. The car was painted a bright French Racing blue, and if you looked at places, like some of the door cuts, where metal panels chafed together, they had these amazing little oval shaped wear patterns, and you could see that it had been repainted a remarkable of times over. It was only about five years old when I got it but had accumulated very high miles. It cost about 2,500 Swiss Francs, I think about $600 at the time.

Lutz introduces the high-performance Cadillac CTS-V to the media. General Motors

If there's a hot car nearby, Lutz won't be far from it, getting comfy here in the Corvette Z06. General Motors

"It also ran on very narrow bias-ply tires and had a lot of positive camber in the rear end. I had it in Switzerland when I was in high school. On wet cobblestones it was lethal. I don't know how many 180-degree spins I took in that thing. It had thin metal bumpers, and the bumper guards were curved out like little horns. Thankfully, I never hit anyone with it. It taught me to drive in situations where traction was marginal. Later on, I had a '62 Corvair Monza—and of course, you know all the fuss that was made over the Corvair's handling back then—but that little VW helped me learn how to drive a rear-engined car with a swing-arm suspension.

Legendary auto executive and all-around car guy Bob Lutz astride the potent Suzuki Hayabusa. Andrew Hetherington/Redux

> ## "On wet cobblestones it was lethal. I don't know how many 180-degree spins I took in that thing."

"I immediately set about putting dual carburetors on it. There were no aftermarket kits back then like they have now, so I rigged up a dual carb setup using motorcycle carburetors, with some sort of cable throttle linkage. Let's not forget that it had really marginal, manual drum brakes too. So the stopping power was about as good as the traction on icy roads. The battery was under the rear seat. Somewhere along the way, the plastic battery cover went missing. There wasn't more than a couple inches between the top of the battery and the metal zigzag-shaped springs in the bottom seat cushion. If you had someone kinda heavy riding back there, the positive and negative poles of the battery would contact the metal springs. Then someone would say, 'Is something burning?' There was more than one instance when we had to empty the car out and pound it into the shower to put the fire out. All of the Porsche Supers at the time had a central 'stinger'-style exhaust system, which I ultimately fit to the VW. It sure sounded great, but couldn't have added more than a few horsepower.

"The car was a great enabler with high school females back then too. This wasn't too long after the end of World War II, and while cars were more and more common in most households in the United States at that time, many European families did without owning transportation. Mass motorization was just gathering steam. I think our high school parking lot was populated by about eight cars; the principal, a few teachers, and me and my VW. There was another student there who had a Porsche. Show off! The VW became increasingly unreliable, so I ultimately dumped it and bought my first new motorcycle."

Lutz's tastes have grown well beyond those of his humble VW days. Well known as a serious car guy, Lutz owns an eclectic variety of cars and motorcycles, including an Aston Martin that once belonged to his father when the family lived in Europe. ∎

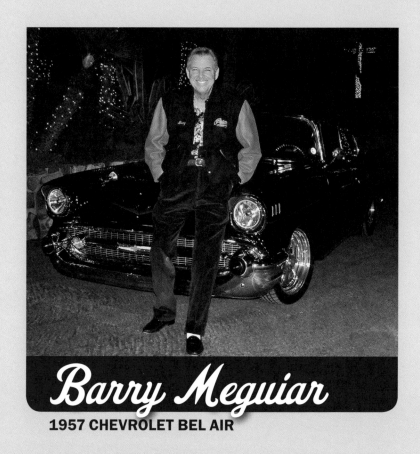

Barry Meguiar

1957 CHEVROLET BEL AIR

Barry Meguiar is president of Meguiar's, one of the world's best known producers of automotive surface and finish care products, born at the turn of the century in Barry Meguiar's great-grandfather's Southern California garage. Meguiar also hosts Meguiar's Car Crazy radio and television shows, which cover the entire automotive enthusiast spectrum Car Crazy is among the most popular automotive programs on television, and Meguiar has become a popular speaker and auto-motive event master of ceremonies.

Ever the enthusiast, Meguiar out cruising his '57 Chevy. This example isn't his actual first car, but a near identical piece that he acquired years later. Barry Meguiar Collection

"It's still my favorite car, and when I drive it I'm 17 years old all over again."

"My first car was a black 1957 Chevy Bel Air Hardtop with the 270-horsepower V-8, with the Duntov Cam option. I bought it in 1958 from Earl Lee's used car lot on Colorado Street in Pasadena, California. I paid $1,850 for it.

"I sold my '57 and bought another car. One night, I was in the middle of the action, in my car at the Bob's Big Boy Drive-In in Pasadena when my old '57 drove in and parked. I heard it before I saw it and I knew when I heard it, it was my car. I knew that very moment that selling it was a mistake. I walked over and told the new owner that I had to have my '57 back, and he sold it back to me.

"I loved the sound of that Duntov Cam bouncing off the storefronts as I drove down Main Street on Balboa Island in California—my favorite place on the planet. I still do it today, only now I set off a trail of car alarms.

"I eventually sold it when I was in college in the early '60s for $1,600. Big mistake, but I didn't know it was going to be the iconic car it is today. Ever since then, I wanted to get it back for good and eventually found a perfect match with the same interior at the Cruisin' for a Cure Car Show in Costa Mesa, California. I bought it for $50,000. It's still my favorite car, and when I drive it (as hot rodding legend and So-Cal Speed Shop owner Pete Chapouris says) I'm 17 years old all over again." ■

McKEEL HAGERTY
1967 Porsche 911S

McKeel Hagerty is the chief executive officer of Hagerty Insurance Agency Inc., headquartered in Traverse City, Michigan. The son of Hagerty founders Frank and Louise Hagerty, he has been working with Hagerty since he could stuff envelopes and answer phones. McKeel's passion for cars began at an early age. McKeel was ultimately appointed president of Hagerty. With the success and growth of the collector car hobby, McKeel thought it was time for Hagerty to give back to the community that served his business so well. In 2003, he established the Hagerty Fund, which evolved into the independent nonprofit Collectors Foundation, providing scholarships to preserve the collector car and boat hobbies through education, library, and museum programs, and youth-oriented activities. McKeel is also a strong legislative advocate for the collector car community.

A young Hagerty toils away on his "teenager restored" 911S, which he still has, and has since been fully and properly restored.
McKeel Hagerty collection

"My first car was a Polo Red 1967 Porsche 911S. A tradition in my family was that each of us kids was allowed to choose the car of our choice to restore in the garage with our dad to drive as our first car. My eldest sister, Kim, restored a 1956 Corvair Lakewood station wagon that was once owned and ice raced by Augie Pabst. Our middle sister, Tammy, restored a 1960 Porsche 356B Roadster; and I restored my 1967 911S.

"The car was in very rusty condition and was purchased together with a 1966 912 from an eccentric old body man and sports car racer when I was 13. We paid $500 each, and he also threw in a wooden Century boat if we agreed to haul it off his beach. What we did with the boat is a separate story. When we picked up the car it was in two major parts. The chassis was resting in a snowbank and the engine, also in the snow, was completely out of the car. It had seized up—not a big surprise, since its only protection against the weather was a wadded up paper towel shoved into the carburetors.

"I did all the work myself under my dad's watchful eye, and the total restoration cost was less than $2,500. But that doesn't begin to tell the story. Since there were no rotisseries back then, I spent months on my back scraping rust into my eyes. I set the car on fire once when I was learning how to do lead work, and I nearly passed out a couple times when I was lying on countless coats of black lacquer paint.

"The car was originally red, but I always liked black cars. So I chose aesthetics over authenticity and decided to paint it black. Technically speaking, the quality of my work was pretty poor. But I put a lot of time into it and got better as time wore on. I will never forget the first time I fired that 911 up—my dad and I hugged each other with tears in our eyes.

"As a boy, I always wanted to be James Bond and drive a cool European sports car. There weren't a lot of Aston Martins in my neighborhood so the 911 suited me just fine. Throughout high school the car was my pride and joy. My best memories were restoring the 911 in the garage with my dad, but I had tons of fun driving it too. I took it to a few PCA track days at the Grattan track in western Michigan where I very quickly learned what oversteer meant! I remember my instructor yelling at me to keep my foot on the gas. Keep my foot *on* the gas?! A teen never imagines hearing those words from a responsible adult. But I did. I swear I spun the thing out so fast on the first hot lap that I could read my own license plate driving by me! I learned pretty quickly that it takes a special kind of courage to drive an early 911 in a competitive way. I was a bit shaky at times, but I worked at it and eventually learned what I and my baby could do. Thankfully, we did it without a crash.

"My engine work left a lot to be desired. The car seemed to go through a set of head gaskets about every 60 days. Another lesson worth learning; I became quite efficient at replacing gaskets. Unfortunately, it is garage work, not roadside repairs. On the road, the gaskets failed at the very worst times, usually when I was trying to impress a young lady. Those who are familiar with 911s—and the aforementioned head gasket problem—know that it creates an oily, smoky mess. Eventually, I learned to change those darned gaskets in about 30 minutes, so I could get back in the dating pool before my reputation suffered further.

"Looking back, I feel lucky to be alive. After driving the 911 for some time, I discovered that I never reinstalled the sway bars, didn't properly attach the fuel tank, and never did manage to stop a couple fuel leaks in the engine compartment. I grenaded the transmission at some point in the early years, rebuilt it, and still managed to scrape up enough money to put on some wheels that had rubber wider than the original bicycle tires. I washed it every time I drove it but didn't really baby it in any other way. I restored it to drive, and it was always a fun driver.

"As life moved on, my 911 was starting to look a little rough around the edges, and eventually I stopped driving it altogether. But it's always been a part of me. About five years ago I enlisted a local shop and proven Porsche experts to do a complete restoration to bring the 911 back to its perfect original condition. What followed was a two-year project that corrected many of the problems I had successfully covered up 20 years earlier. When they were done I had a car in show-winning form.

"For what it is worth, I'm sure I now own the world's most expensive 1967 911S. I'm thinking of starting a support group. But all I see when I look at it is memories—a lot of very good memories."

Hagerty may own one of the world's most expensively restored early 911Ss, but it is undoubtedly among the best as well. He freely admits that its value to him is in the story, not just the car. ■

Hagerty back in the day, with his now black 911 all shined up and ready for a date. McKeel Hagerty collection

An only slightly older Hagerty stands proudly with his first car, a rare and valuable short wheelbased 911S, now restored and repainted in its original red. McKeel Hagerty collection

PETER BROCK
1949 MG TC and 1946 Ford

Peter Brock's life and automotive career have taken many paths. After school, a young Brock worked at General Motors' design studio. He later joined Shelby American, where he designed the international sports car championship-winning Shelby Daytona Cobra Coupe. His Brock Racing Enterprises Datsun 510s took the "under 2.5-liter" Trans-Am racing title in 1971 and 1972. Brock remains involved in many author motorsport and automotive design enterprises, and also works as a professional automotive journalist and photographer.

"As a child of divorced parents, I didn't have much masculine guidance until we moved to Sausalito, a small town just across the Golden Gate from San Francisco. I was in the seventh grade at that time, about 12 years old. My next door neighbor, Mr. Warren, had an MG TC. This wasn't just any TC, but one he'd built to race! In 1949, a 19-inch wire-wheeled MG was a rarity. I'd never seen anything like a sports car prior to that point, and the fact that he'd occasionally take me for a ride was just about the coolest thing I'd ever experienced. I lived for the moment when he'd get home, slide the garage door open, and I could help him change the oil or wash the car. After that we'd have to 'test it,' blasting through the then-empty, hilly back roads of Marin County; the MG's long, flat hood mirroring the trees and sky with a constantly changing pattern that slid by on its polished surface with an almost mystical cadence.

"Being right-hand drive, I got to sit on the 'driver's side' and give the 'go' signal if the road was clear when we came up behind another car. With the windscreen folded flat and its straight pipe blaring, that MG was the epitome of an early SCCA racer, and I knew then that someday I'd have to have one. At the end of these eye-watering, ear-shattering runs, we'd usually stop at the Sports Car Center, a random collection of quonset-hutted repair shops on the edge of the mud flats bordering the San Francisco Bay. There were always other racers there, working on their cars or making plans for the next event. No one had a trailer in those days. The informal group would just meet early on Friday mornings and head out on the back roads to Cotati, Stockton, Reno, or maybe the 'big one,' down in Monterey at Pebble Beach; the whole group rat-racing their noisy, cut-down, cycle-fendered creations in preparation for the real thing the next day. Being half their age, I felt privileged with their acceptance, and my life soon focused on racing and things mechanical instead of the usual after-school activities like sports. In time, I talked my way into an after-school job at the Sports Car Center, sweeping floors, cleaning tools, and trying to learn as much as I could. I'd already decided that I was going to have a TC by the time I was 16 and could get my license.

"The best part about working there was Nadeau Bourgeoult, an irascible old Frenchman who did body work. It took some time, but over many months he began to understand my interest in his skill was really serious. I watched him build, from a bare set of TC rails, an alloy-bodied, supercharged 'special,' the fastest and most exotic form of road racer in those days. Never having seen anything fabricated from raw materials, it was a fascinating, educational experience that changed, forever, my concept of what was possible. Old Nadeau never

A young Peter Brock and his "right hooker" MG. Right-hand drive cars were relatively rare in the U.S. in the late 1940s and early 1950s.
Peter Brock Collection

said much, but one quiet Saturday afternoon, he fired the engine and made ready for a run in the hills. The combined sounds of the supercharger and engine made conversation impossible. As he leaned over the engine, manually controlling the throttle, he turned, peered over his cracked, weld-spattered glasses, and nodded to the space alongside the driver's seat. I clambered in and sat on the bare floor of the cockpit, watching the instruments as he warmed the engine. The tach needle moved in precise incremental jumps matching the high-pitched scream of the Roots blower. Combined with the sound and resonance of the megaphone, exiting right under my seat, the whole chassis seemed feral, yet precisely and mechanically constrained by its master. Tiny grains of sand on the aluminum floor would dance and spin in the sunlight in concert with the rise and fall of the engine's speed, and then we were off!

"Conversation was impossible and Nadeau seldom looked over. He was concentrating on keeping his alloy rocket pointed exactly where he wanted, and I soon realized he wasn't controlling our line on the narrow two-lane road with just the steering wheel! On a long sweeper, headed back toward the shop, I remember looking down at the pavement, mere inches below the alloy sheet of the belly pan that supported me. The just-visible edge of the rear tire was a black blur on the grey edge of the road. Had it moved outward even an inch we would have been in the dirt. I looked up and realized the nose of the car was pointed slightly across the road and we were held there, suspended in a long drift just by the slippage of the tires and Nadeau's pressure on the throttle! That exact moment was a life changing incident.

"Every mechanical experience of those formative days was filed away along with every penny I could save. My only goal was having my own TC. By the time I was 16, I had saved almost enough to acquire a broken-engined '49 that had been impatiently shunted away in the back of the shop by its disgruntled, insensitive owner, who obviously had no regard for things automotive. He'd forgotten, somehow, to check the coolant and had blown the engine. By then, MG had introduced its newer, softer, more mechanically sophisticated TD, but even if I could have afforded one, it didn't have the same crisp esthetic, classic appeal, of the earlier model, especially that dust-covered, light

Brock's future as an automotive designer was already beginning to show up in the mild mods he'd given his 1946 Ford. Notice the padded top, subtle dechroming, and lack of running boards. *Peter Brock Collection*

Notice that the factory hood is gone and that the front visage has been fully restyled on Brock's Ford as he hangs out here with his gang, likely in Carmel, California. The hood's absence likely indicates that the original flathead had by then been swapped with a Cadillac overhead valve V-8, creating a mighty Ford-illac. *Peter Brock Collection*

A proud Brock beams with the trophy he and the Ford earned at the National Roadster Show. Peter Brock Collection

blue one that languished in the back room! I'd had my eye on that car for months and was completely focused on the possibilities should possession become a reality.

"With some parental help, I was finally able to swing the deal and buy the car. My mechanic friends in the shop helped rebuild the engine using some cast off parts they'd collected for me during the previous months. When we finally fired the engine, I couldn't have been happier. I'd already spent weeks going over every nut and bolt on the chassis and stripping the interior of every bit of extra weight and the convertible top. Real racers didn't have radios, carpets, and tops, and I'd vowed my MG would never have those. The body panel just below the radiator had been damaged. Nadeau straightened it and I had him paint it white so the car's livery would match America's international racing colors of blue and white. With its center-zipped tonneau covering the passenger seat, it was as close to a production racer as I could make it. I could carry my sleeping bag and some tools, in the space behind the seats, so every race weekend was an adventure. I spent many a rainy northern California night sleeping under the MG's long sweeping fenders. Since several of my friends from the Sports Car Center raced, I was seldom alone and had access to the pits and a chance to learn about racing from the inside.

"Later, when I moved away from my road-racing friends in Sausalito and started high school farther south in Menlo Park, I found a whole new group of younger car-guy friends my age. No one in that group seemed to know much about sports cars, and as much as I loved my MG, I found I was just as interested in hopped-up, flathead Fords; especially when that engine was nestled in a light set of Model A rails with a dropped front axle and channeled coupe or roadster body! Damn, hot rods were really cool; a real American automotive art form!

"My MG didn't have a chance in the midnight drag racing scene, and I soon found myself looking for something faster. The opportunity came when I found a half completed '46 Ford convert on a used car lot in San Francisco. It was love at first sight. Someone with real talent had chopped and channeled that piece and I wasn't about to let it disappear. The MG was traded almost straight across with no sense of loss, and I started on the Ford, eventually building it into an Oakland Roadster Show winner. Later it got a Cadillac engine—one of the first non-flathead conversions of that era. Eventually I sold it to get cash to go the Art Center School to study automotive design. Those were great years. None of it would ever have happened, though, without that life changing ride in the old Frenchman's supercharged TC special.

"Thanks, Nadeau. Wherever you are, I owe you."

Brock remains involved in many other motorsport and automotive design enterprises, and also works as a professional automotive journalist and photographer. ■

BEAU BOECKMANN
1965 Mercedes-Benz 220 SE

Boeckmann grew up in the car business, and possesses the car collection to back it up. Beau Boeckmann collection

Beau Boeckmann grew up in the automobile business under the tutelage of his legendary father, Bert Boeckmann, the number one Ford dealer in the world, who was also a pioneering force in dealer customization in the mid-1960s. Bert helped launch a national craze with his "Surfer Vans," 4x4 trucks, and other vehicles. They called the process "Galpinizing." So to young Beau, customization was the norm. In fact, his first project was at the age of 15 with a 1965 Mercedes his grandmother had left him.

Beau was born in Los Angeles, California, and earned his Bachelor of Science degree from USC in 1992, where he was on the Dean's list, and majored in Business Administration with an emphasis in USC's renowned entrepreneurship program. His education, coupled with his creativity and natural affinity for automobiles, was the perfect combination.

Today, Beau Boeckmann is vice president of Galpin Motors, Inc.—the number one Ford dealer in the world for the past 20 years. Additionally, he is president of Galpin Premier Collection, which includes Aston Martin, Jaguar, Volvo, Lincoln, Mercury, Mazda, Spyker, and Lotus, and is president of Galpin Auto Sports (GAS), which is a complete design and customization organization with the ability to customize all makes and models of vehicles. GAS became world famous in 2005 when MTV began filming Pimp My Ride on site where Beau was not only on-screen talent, but consulting producer. One of the most *famous segments was created for Earth Day and featured Governor Schwarzenegger revealing a 1965 Chevy Impala that ran on pure B100 biodiesel and had over 850 horsepower!*

"My grandmother willed this car to me when she passed away in the early '80s. For my 16th birthday, I restored it and customized it. So really, I got it when I was 15-and-a-half when I started driving, and the restoration was completed with my 16th birthday. After the restoration, it was lacquer black over black with vinyl leopard-skin inserts. As tacky as it sounds, it came out really cool. The restoration cost was my 16th birthday gift from my family.

"When I was a little kid, my favorite color was green. I loved, loved green. My grandmother used to drive up every summer from Arkansas to California with this car. Every summer, I would see my grandma arrive in the car, and as it was green over green, I absolutely

"It's the last one I'd sell," says Boeckmann of his first car, his grandmother's Benz. *Beau Boeckmann collection*

loved it. Since she knew how much the car meant to me, she gave it to me in her will.

"I was looking for a way to make it really cool and custom. I wasn't sure what color to paint, until I saw a magazine story, I think it was *LIFE* magazine that had a Cadillac with leopard-skin interior. When I went to our reconditioning shop to get the materials, they didn't have what I wanted, so they suggested red with white and red interior, which I thought looked kind of hideous. They suggested some styles, and none of them were working. Eventually we realized that they had thought I said *zebra* instead of leopard. Turns out they happened to have a roll of leopard-skin-patterned vinyl in the back of the shop from the 1950s. I drove it through most of my high school years.

"What I loved most about it was the family history that gave life to the car. I was very close to my grandmother, and that was our bond. I love that automobile. Still, to this day, it is the last material possession I would ever sell. I also love the fact that even though my ideas for it sounded pretty tacky, it came out pretty cool. I've had multiple offers over the years from people who have wanted to buy the car.

"To me it's priceless. If we had to sell every car at Galpin, that's the last car I would sell."

One of Beau's favorite projects was Ed "Big Daddy" Roth's *Orbitron*. Built in 1962, the vehicle had been lost for 35 years until it was found outside of an adult bookstore in Juarez, Mexico, where it was being used as a dumpster. Not only did GAS rebuild and restore this rare creation to concourse standards, but the project also reassembled much of the team that actually worked on the show car in the 1960s. Boeckmann also maintains a fine collection of rare and expensive Shelby Mustangs. ■

"Turns out they happened to have a roll of leopard-skin-patterned vinyl in the back of the shop from the 1950s."

GEORGE BARRIS
1925 Buick

The self-proclaimed King of the Kustomizers needs little introduction. George Barris, along with his late brother Sam, are among the pioneers of the custom car trend that exploded in Southern California just after World War II. Barris took his chop-and-channeling, nosing-and-decking auto body craft to nearby Hollywood, and created some of the most memorable television and movie cars ever. They include the Munster Coach used on The Munsters *television show, the Greased Lightning 1946 Ford convertible from the movie* Grease, *and one of the most famous star cars of all time, the original Batmobile made famous by the 1960s small-screen smash series,* Batman. *Always the promoter, and well into his 80s as of this writing, Barris is still working, and is a popular guest at numerous car shows and events where the line for his autograph is always long.*

"My first car was a hand-me-down 1925 Buick from my parents. I was just 13 years old."

Apparently the seed for personalizing or customizing cars—a unique notion in America at the time—was already germinating in the young Barris' mind. But there was no "automotive aftermarket" as we know it today. Anything done to an automobile was the product of ingenuity, handy work, and making do with available materials.

"I went to the hardware store," Barris recalls. "I bought some house paint and put scallops on the fenders and hood."

"Scalloping" is just one of many custom painting techniques that Barris and others employed during the heyday of customizing, roughly 1947 though the mid-1960s, although it made a return during the van craze of the 1970s.

"I then went to Woolworth's five and dime," Barris continues, "and got some foxtails for my radio antenna. Moving on from there, I went to a kitchen store to get some shallow [cooking] pans to use as my hubcaps."

Parts are where you find them. These simplistic techniques served Barris for decades, especially on television and movie cars,

"When I took my car to school, I was a real 'king' because my car was customized."

where close-up detail isn't as important as overall look, color, and wow factor. "When I got home from there, I went to the cabinets in my mother's bedroom and took off the knobs, and put them on the grille of my Buick. It really looked beautiful!"

Look at many of Barris' 1960s and 1970s creations built for a role in a film or series, and you'll see all manner of hardware store bits. Scoops, grilles, tubing—even kitchen knobs found their way into a variety of wacky Barris projects.

"When I took my car to school, I was a real 'king' because my car was customized."

In order to add a little twist to the notion of customizing, Barris changed the "c" to a "k." It is a term still in use today to describe his work. Indeed, his company in Burbank, California (just around the corner from numerous Hollywood studios) is still named Barris Kustom Industries.

Barris doesn't recall what his folks paid for that humble 1925 Buick, but given that it was little more than a used car in the years prior to World War II, it couldn't have been much. He also doesn't remember how long he kept it or what happened to it. No photos exist, so many elements of the story are lost to time. But there's one important aspect of it that Barris remembers with absolute clarity.

"That night, Mom couldn't open any of the cabinets in her bedroom because all the knobs were gone. Typical teenaged boy. I was grounded. But ultimately, my parents supported what my brother Sam and I [were doing], and I was able to buy a '32 Ford Roadster—to customize, of course."

From bolting kitchen cabinet knobs to the grille of an old Buick to creating the Batmobile, Barris' trip through autodom has been a long and interesting ride, to be sure. ∎

Barris (right front, wearing goggles) and his boys hard at work on an early customization job. *George Barris collection*

Barris tops off the fluids in the Munster Coach, one of the great TV car creations with which he is most associated. *George Barris collection*

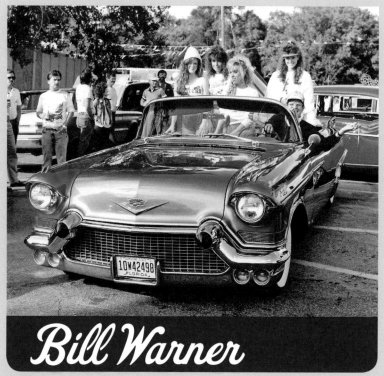

Bill Warner

1961 BUICK LeSABRE

Bill Warner is an automotive enthusiast of the first order. A resident of Jacksonville, Florida, Warner is a professional motorsport photographer, car collector and restorer, vintage racer, and founder and chairman of the Amelia Island Concours d'Elegance. Bill Warner owns and has owned an interesting and eclectic roster of fine automobiles.

Warner is the consummate automotive racing enthusiast, collector, photographer, and concours founder and promoter. He and his El Dorado seem to be enjoying their visit to a nearby Hooters. Bill Warner collection

> *"One time on old U.S. 17, I passed an unmarked Georgia State Trooper who was chasing someone else at the time. He was not amused."*

"My first car was my father's hand-me-down 1961 Buick LeSabre two-door hardtop. Unbeknownst to the family, I use to drag race it at the Walterboro Drag Strip in South Carolina while I was in school at the Citadel in nearby Charleston. No one except Lenny Kennedy (who won the National Championship in an Invicta) ever drag raced a Buick. I'd put 40 psi in the front tires, pop the hubcaps, take the air cleaner off, and run it H Stock Automatic. Because it had Dynaflow, it never shifted; just made this moaning dying moose sound, 'Barroooooooooooooooooooooo.' It became known as the 'Blue Baroo.' Even won a few meets until they decided they didn't want a Buick winning and bumped me to H Stock [manual shift].

"The Blue Baroo and I became famous around Charleston and Jacksonville as I always tried to break my previous Charleston to Jacksonville run by a minute. One time on old U.S. 17, I passed an unmarked Georgia State Trooper who was chasing someone else at the time. He was not amused. Stopped me and the car he was chasing and said, 'Son, welcome to McIntosh County, Georgia. I've stopped people going faster than you, and I have stopped more than two people before, but that's the first time I've ever been passed while chasing someone else.'" ∎

CHIP FOOSE
1956 Ford F-100 Pickup

Chip Foose is a well-known automotive designer, customizer, hot rod and custom builder, and the host of the popular television series, Overhaulin'. Chip's career profile is impressive. In 1986 he was staff designer/fabricator for the ASHA Corporation, eventually becoming director of design in 1989. Chip was responsible for conceptualizing new proprietary ideas and fabrication of prototypes for several major manufacturers. Other work has included Stehrenberger Design as an automotive designer, creating illustrations, and conceptual models; Baker Sportronics; chief designer and fabricator of electric vehicles used in the NFL and NBA; and of course, going to work with his father at Project Design, designing and building street rods, customs, studio vehicles, and show cars for films such as Blade Runner, RoboCop, *and* Gone in 60 Seconds.

"I grew up in Goleta, California. That truck was originally owned by Goleta Auto Parts—they used to deliver parts to my dad's shop (Project Design) back in the day. My dad bought it in 1968, and it was his daily commuter and shop truck. When I was a kid, we did some remodeling work to my family's home, which included a new driveway. We mixed all the cement for the driveway in the bed of that truck! [Custom car show promoter] R. G. Canning used to have a big car show at the Earl Warren Fairgrounds, and two weeks before the show in 1975, my dad said, 'Hey, let's build the F-100 into a show truck and take it to Canning's.' So I helped him, and we took it apart and restored and entered it into the show. We took it to Richard Jeffries to have the interior done. I remember taking it to his shop one night— I'll never forget how cold it was because we had taken all the windows out of it. I learned how to drive in this truck. I used to follow him to work in my bike, and then he'd let me drive home.

"We finished it just in time and made it to the show, and won best truck of the event. It appeared in *Hot Rod* magazine a few times. And then in 1978, when I turned 16, I bought it from my father for $2,000. After its brief career as a show vehicle, Dad put it back into every day service. It still looked good, but it was wearing, so I repainted it again in candy root beer brown—with 11 gallons of lacquer. That paint job ultimately cracked pretty bad, so in 1984, I stripped it and redid it again. It's always been my baby, and any time anything ever happened to it, I fixed it right away. I never wanted to see it or drive it damaged in any way. Then, I had to sell it to help pay to attend Art Center [College of Design].

"Three years later, my father repurchased it from the guy I sold it to. Then, in 1992, I bought it back from dad. So it's been in the family from 1968 to the present, with the exception of the three years we didn't own it while I was in school. I will quietly admit that when I was in high school, I engineered and built an electrically operated canvas bed cover for it. Once or twice, my girlfriend and I would hop in the back, and since there was a switch back there, I could close up the cover, and nobody knew we were there.

"When I went to work for Boyd Coddington, I had a company vehicle, so I parked it on the side of my house, and it was ruined just

Foose poses with a customized Foose Edition F-150. He's built countless customs and won crateloads of trophies and awards for his great design and top-notch craftsmanship. Ford

The body mods given to Foose's '56 "Effie" are subtle but effective; the all black paint, huge rolling stock, and aggressive stance complete the spot-on custom look.
Chip Foose collection

sitting out in the elements. Then, my father and the producers of The Learning Channel's *Overhaulin'* television program, decided to 'steal' my truck and give it a complete makeover. They did, and my father ran the crew that redesigned and remodeled the truck. They fooled me, but not completely, because when the truck disappeared from our shop, so did a large Foose sign. I thought, 'Somebody is messin' with me.' Why would a regular car thief take a sign showing where they stole a truck from? They wouldn't. So I suspected something was up. With some inside help, perhaps.

"After six months, we didn't hear a word about it, so I figured it was really gone. Then *Overhaulin'* producer Bud Brutsman told me that Jack Roush asked if I would help unveil his new Ford 427 V-8 at the SEMA show in Las Vegas, and of course said yes. At the unveiling, I cut the ribbon and turned around to see what everyone clapping at and taking photos of. It turned out to be my truck, of course, fully restored and chopped and reproportioned to match drawings I had done. I looked at the back, there was my license plate—FOOSED—the

The finely detailed custom fabrication work that Foose Design team members are noted for are evident in the reworked tailgate and custom made rear bumper they gave Foose's F-100.
Chip Foose collection

original meaning of which is *Foose* Design, the company I started in 1984 in Santa Barbara. I saw it standing there, and asked if it was really mine. He said that it was. I'll never ever forget that moment, and I still love the way it came out. They even put one of Roush's new 427s in it. It'll never be sold again. Hopefully, my son Brock will want it as something we can play with together, although I may pull out the 427 when it's time for him to learn how to drive."

Hopefully young Brock Foose will be aware of the family legacy with which he'll likely be entrusted, and chooses something else in the event he's in need of a cement mixer. ■

"We mixed all the cement for the driveway in the bed of that truck!"

No stock workhorse cabin for Foose's F-100. Custom leatherwork
adorns the seats, door panels, and upper dashboard. The steering
wheel is a 1940 Ford style piece, popular with customizers and hot
rodders. Chip Foose Collection

Foose at the annual SEMA trade show with another Foose-customized Ford. Ford

Foose among blue oval legends and heroes at the SEMA show, with Edsel Ford II and Carroll Shelby. Ford

3

Practice Makes Perfect...
Driving

STARS
OF STAGE,
SCREEN AND
SOUND

JAY LENO
1934 Ford pickup

Known the world over as the host of NBC's The Tonight Show, *and a formidable stand-up comedic talent, Jay Leno is one of Hollywood truest car guys. His compound, not far from the NBC studios where he tapes America's top late-night talk show in Burbank, California, is affectionately named the Big Dog Garage. Its several buildings are filled with many dozens of cars and who knows how many motorcycles. His facilities include a comprehensive restoration shop and library, and the knowledgeable Leno can be found there on most weekends, up to his elbows in one restoration project or another. His massive collection is eclectic and varied, demonstrating his particular penchants for Duesenbergs, Bentleys, and Lamborghinis. Leno can often be seen driving to work in a pint-sized Fiat Topolino one day, and a McLaren F1 exotic the next. He owns vehicles powered by steam, by aircraft engines, turbines, even a tank engine. A frequent automotive columnist in magazines, Jay Leno is also a host of the Pebble Beach Concours d'Elegance.*

"I was 14 years old at the time. I was working at McDonald's and other summer jobs, and I remember one day when my dad and I drove past a gas station in Redding, Massachusetts. This truck was parked next to the station, and it was for sale. I walked into the station and asked 'How much?' The guy said '$350.' Being the shrewd negotiator that I was, I said 'Okay—I'll take it.' I scraped together the money, and my dad drove it back to the house since I was too young to drive it home myself.

"At the time, my mom had a Ford Falcon and my dad had a Ford Galaxie. Both were automatics. I used to lie in bed and have nightmares: 'What if I can't drive a stick? What if I'm one of those guys that's just not coordinated enough to do it?' I'd wake up in the middle of the night wondering what I was going to do if I couldn't drive a stick because, of course, the truck had a manual transmission. Ah, the stupid kid things that you worry about.

"It needed a lot of work. I spent two years sanding, priming, and getting it ready for the day I got my license. I grew up in Andover,

Leno smiles a knowing smile in the "shop" area of his massive Burbank, California, Big Dog Garage complex. His shop includes a paint booth and an impressive array of machine tools, and he and his small crew of hot rodders and craftsmen perform many of their own builds and restorations. *The Tonight Show with Jay Leno*

Massachusetts, and it was a little more rural at the time. We had about three acres. Our house was set way back on the property, and we had a long driveway. Although I never snuck the car out, I used to drive up the driveway, shift into second, and then hit the brakes. Then I'd back all the way up and do it again. I must have done that 1,000 times. I still have a crick in my neck from looking over my shoulder while backing the truck up that driveway. It's probably the only vehicle in the world with as many miles on it in reverse as it had in any of the forward gears. I would do this all day long. Then I'd fiddle with it, adjust the carburetor, whatever. Finally my mother would say, 'Would you please stop backing up and down the driveway.'"

The year 1934 was a great time for the Ford Motor Company. Henry Ford had put the world on its ear (again) by bringing out an affordable line of V-8-powered automobiles. Up until 1932 and the debut of Ford's venerable "flathead," V-8 power was reserved for

> *"I'd wake up in the middle of the night wondering what I was going to do if I couldn't drive a stick because, of course, the truck had a manual transmission. Ah, the stupid kid things that you worry about."*

expensive cars, and thus, mostly for the well-to-do. Several Fords of that era, particularly the even-numbered models (1932, '34, '36, and '40) have become sought after classics. Leno's 1934 pickup had a sweetheart-shaped grille similar to those on the passenger car models, wire wheels, a three-speed manual transmission, and the above-mentioned flathead V-8 engine.

"I finally got my driver's license," continues Jay, "and after all the sanding and priming, I painted the Ford burgundy maroon. I remember taking it to this paint shop, and the guy said 'Ooh, it'll be at least $100 to paint that thing,' which seemed like a lot of money at the time. I did some more sanding and prep, and the guy was able to cut it to $80. He did a great job.

"As a gift, my parents redid the bench seat in black Naugahyde. So it's all done, it looked great, and I'm driving the car around. One day, my buddy got in, was fooling around, and slammed the driver's side door. This was before safety glass, so you know what happened: the window shattered into pieces. I had no driver's door glass. I still had to take it to school, and I remember one day, I was sitting in math class, and I could see the car in the parking lot. Of course, it began to rain. And then it was pouring rain. All I could think about was my new Naugahyde interior being ruined by all this water. Here comes another nightmare.

"After about 20 minutes, I'd lost all hope for my upholstery. Then I looked out the window and saw my dad. He'd left the office, and he and my mom had picked up a huge sheet of plastic. I'll never forget it. Sitting in math class watching these two 'old people'—who were probably younger then than I am now—struggling while trying to cover my car with plastic. I started to cry. They were out there in the rain for probably 20 minutes, trying to cover my truck so it wouldn't be damaged. I'll never forget that.

"I always liked that car, and I had it for quite a while. Then I traded it in for a Datsun 1600 sports car with a four-speed transmission because my truck had begun to seem like 'how old fashioned is that?' I wanted to get something cool and something the girls would like (or at least so I thought)."

It's easy to see why the tall, handsome, single young Leno wanted a sports car. In general size, shape, and purpose, the Datsun roadster resembled an MGB—potentially more attractive to young women than an old truck from the 1930s.

"I've tried to track down my old Ford truck, and I'm sure it's still around the Massachusetts area somewhere. Hopefully we'll be reunited some day." ∎

Leno out in the California Desert with his Blastolene Brothers "tank car," appropriately named given the Chrysler tank engine it relies on for power. The Tonight Show with Jay Leno

Alan de Cadenet

1928 MG

London-born Alan de Cadenet is a consummate enthusiast of all motorized things. A former professional sports car racer and race car builder credited with a third place overall finish at the 24 Hours of Le Mans in 1976 in a Ford Cosworth–powered De Cadenet Lola T380. "De Cad" now occupies much of his time as writer and popular automotive television personality, perhaps known best for the Victory by Design series, which he hosts.

"Hmm, interesting. Teenage boys need all the help they can get."

"My first car was a motorcycle, as there was no way I could either afford a car or even drive one. But after difficulties persuading genteel young ladies that being a passenger on a motorcycle wasn't really as dangerous as they had been told, and that one didn't actually feel the cold after the first few hundred yards, I knew I needed a car and needed it badly.

"My savior was a 1928 MG M-type—a tiny, blue, open-cockpit machine with zero weather protection. The owner wanted five guineas for it. That's five pounds, five shillings, in good old fashioned British pre-decimal money. Usually only horses and serious works of art were sold in guineas, but the owner of this car said it was so special that it could only be sold in guineas.

"It had taken me ages to work up from a BSA Bantam two-stroke to a Royal Enfield 650, and I was sorry to see the latter go, but the four pounds I got for it was the deposit for the MG.

"Bear in mind, this was all some time ago, and things like driving licenses and insurance weren't at the top of my list. A week after clamping eyes on her for the first time, I completed payment and the owner then said in a clipped, upper-class accent, 'Well, my boy, now she's yours. I'm going to show a special secret that's installed on her.' He pointed to a small electrical switch just down on the right of the dashboard. 'See that?' he said. 'When you have a girl with you, and you're down a leafy lane, you click the switch and the engine stops.' I was initially somewhat puzzled, until he explained that it was then that she might need a cuddle to keep warm. Hmm, interesting. Teenage boys need all the help they can get.

"I learned plenty from that little car, and not just how to keep the 850cc overhead cam engine in tune and get the brakes to pull up square. I was offered 10 pounds for it some months later. 'Make that guineas and she's yours,' I said."

DeCadenet has retired from professional motorsport as a driver, but still participates in vintage racing and owns numerous old motorcycles. Since hanging up his helmet and goggles, he's become an accomplished motoring writer and concours judge. ■

Opposite: "DeCad" isn't afraid to roll up his sleeves, or take off his shirt, when a motor needs some fettling. This is the muffler off of his Royal Enfield motorcycle. Alan DeCadenet collection

RICH CHRISTENSEN
1965 Chevrolet Chevelle

Rich Christensen is a television producer from New Hampton, Iowa. Christensen went to the University of Northern Iowa *and is best known as the creator, lead executive producer, and host of the reality drag racing shows* Pinks *and* Pinks: All Out, *as well other automotive-based television programming. In his own words: "I create and sell television shows for a living. There is almost a 99% failure rate doing what I do. I wake up each day with one goal—to fight as hard as humanly possible for that 1% opportunity."*

"We lived New Hampton, Iowa, [a town of] about 3,500 people. I was that kid who got good grades, I was into sports, and I've only had two sips of beer in my life.

The mismatched rolling stock on his Chevelle didn't bother Christensen a bit. He just never got around to acquiring another set of Keystone mags for the rear axle. Rich Christensen collection

Christensen today, in his traditional starting line pose ready to drop his arms and light off another episode of his drag racing reality show, Pinks. Rich Christensen collection

"As a reward, Dad began looking for a car for me the day after I got my driver's license in 1980. He ran a small Culligan water-softener business so we didn't have a lot of money. He would look for cars while out on his delivery route. Understand that this is a very rural area, hundreds of thousands of acres of cornfields.

"One day, he found this '65 Chevelle two-door hardtop behind some farmer's barn. It was white, all jacked up, and had been left out in the open. My dad asked if he wanted to sell it, and their negotiations went on for about a month and a half. He finally told me that he'd found the car he wants me to have. I had no idea what to expect. He took me out to look at it, and it was the ugliest thing you've ever seen. The floors were rusted all the way through, mostly because the owner was using it as a fishing vehicle. I opened up the trunk, and it was full of newspapers and dirt, because he used to breed his nightcrawlers in there.

"My dad gave him $300—plus a used automatic soft water unit! We knew another farmer who had some barn space, and he let me store the car and work on it there. The first time I drove it was to take

> "The floors were rusted all the way through, mostly because the owner was using it as a fishing vehicle. I opened up the trunk, and it was full of newspapers and dirt, because he used to breed his nightcrawlers in there."

it to this place, and because those floors were rusted clean through, I was looking at the ground rushing underneath me. There were so many holes in it.

"We'd go out there every single weekend and just keep cleaning it, tearing it down, and working on it. We did it together, and my dad just loved every second of it. I was just a kid and didn't realize the value of the experience at the time, but he really enjoyed it.

"We had the upholstery done in that red crushed velvet that was popular at the time—hilarious. It had a 250-cubic-inch, straight six-cylinder with three-on-the-tree trans, and it just ran and ran and ran. No power steering, no power brakes.

"I couldn't afford to have matching rims. You'll notice that there are two different types of rims on the car. Those Keystone Classic mags I had came off a wrecked Chevy, and I thought I'd hit the lottery. I painted it black and would just shine that thing like you can't believe. I took it to the prom, took it on a lot of first dates. Let's just say that all kinds of firsts happened in that car.

"It ran straight and true down the road. I could let go of the steering wheel and it would run for five miles before I had to touch it again. It wasn't fast, but it had adequate power. I'd put snow tires on it during winter, and learned how to 'rock' a car out of the snow when it got stuck.

"We used to pack all my buddies in and go cruising, just like in *American Graffiti*. We'd go up and down the Main Street what seemed like 800 times in a night. Everybody would pitch in a buck for gas, then we'd drive to Charles City, which was about 18 miles away and home to the nearest McDonalds. Think Mayberry RFD with a Chevy straight six.

"I drove it for six years and never did anything other than change the oil. Once we got it all done up, I never had any problems with it. I kept it up as nice as I could, but we never did put new metal in the floors, so after all those Iowa winters, the rust had really attacked the bottom of the car.

"It was the car that took me through high school and college, and then I sold it just before I moved to Los Angeles. I thought I'd blown the engine, so I gave it to a friend of mine's brother who was happy to come take it away. It took a mechanic about 20 minutes to figure out what was wrong, nothing major, and he got it running great again. They drove it another five or so years, and I think it ultimately ended up in a demolition derby.

"I look at that photo and was so fond of that thing. My old Chevy was a real tank, the farmer's fishing car. Every time I see one driving down the road, every time a '65 Chevelle comes up to the starting line on *Pinks*, it takes me back to being 16 again. It was just the coolest thing, the greatest car of my life, and I loved it."

Christensen has faced a number of 1965 Chevelles on the starting line during various episodes of *Pinks*, and quietly wonders if any of them could be his old Chevy. ■

> "It was just the coolest thing, the greatest car of my life, and I loved it."

Robert "R. J." Wagner

1936 FORD THREE-WINDOW COUPE

A young Robert Wagner with another classic Ford, in this case, a '55 Thunderbird, not his much-loved '36. Everett Collection

Robert Wagner was born in Detroit, so it's no wonder he developed a certain affinity for automobiles, and that several of his favorite cars were Fords. Wagner is perhaps best known for male lead Jonathan Hart in the long-running television series Hart-to-Hart. *His film career began with several uncredited roles in the early 1950s. Another successful television run was his role as Alexander Mundy in the late 1960s crime series* It Takes a Thief. *He continues to be an in-demand and popular film actor, as is well known to younger audiences as "Number Two" in the Austin Powers film trilogy. Wagner recently published is autobiography entitled* Pieces of My Heart: A Life.

"I saw what became my first car on a used car lot, and I paid $300 for it in 1946. I was 16 and I earned the money by grooming horses, raking leaves, and several other of the usual teenaged money-making pursuits. I loved this car—it was sensational! It was a light, pale blue, and had 'ripple' disk hubcaps and fender skirts. It was a great-looking car. I recall having a lot dates in that car—I tried to have as many as I could. Didn't every 16 year old?

"It was a great-looking car.
I recall having a lot of dates
in that car—I tried to have
as many as I could.
Didn't every 16 year old?"

"*I like the fact that it was simple, and anybody anywhere could work on it. When one of today's complicated cars breaks down, you use your cell phone to call someone to come and pick it up.*"

"I used to pack it full of friends and go out to the desert or up to Lake Arrowhead. It ran really well; never overheated. I took really good care of it. It was always clean and it ran really good. I like the fact that it was simple, and anybody anywhere could work on it. When one of today's complicated cars breaks down, you use your cell phone to call someone to come and pick it up.

"It was basically stock. I had Edmunds heads and dual exhausts—it sounded great. The only problem with those pipes was that it was loud. Thank goodness there was a little downhill run to my house so I could coast it in late at night if I was out past curfew. I'd shut the engine down, put the car in neutral, and coast into the driveway without those pipes announcing my arrival.

"I had it a couple years, and then traded it for a '32 Ford roadster, which I ran at the dry lakes at 109 mph, which I thought was pretty hot. It had a '41 Ford V-8 in it; it was good looking too and pretty fast for what it was. Then that went for a '39 Ford convertible, which was also very nice. But it being my first car, there was something extra special about that '36." ∎

Robert Wagner never built much of a reputation as a "car guy," although he is an avid aviator and must have been a motorcycle enthusiast at one time. Robert Phillips/Everett Collection

MIKE JOY

1960 Chevrolet Impala Convertible

Mike Joy is a professional motorsports broadcaster. His face and voice is known around the world for having broadcast some of the most important victories and tragedies in NASCAR. He was in victory lane when an overwhelmed and overjoyed Darrell Waltrip realized he's finally won the Daytona 500. Joy was also one of the commentators at work when Dale Earnhardt suffered his fatal crash at Daytona in 2001. He's a serious enthusiast, having owned an eclectic variety of collector cars over the years, and he's tried his hand at sports car racing, having competed at the 24 Hours of Daytona in a GTS class Camaro in 1993.

"My first car was a 1960 Chevrolet Impala convertible. Its 283-cubic-inch small-block V-8 had a two-barrel carb, Powerglide two-speed automatic trans, power steering and brakes, and AM radio. It was horizon blue metallic with blue interior, white top, and white Impala side trim. It was sold new by a Chevy dealer that is still in business in the center of Avon, Connecticut.

"A friend of mine and I saw it on the lot at the Mercury dealership in Windsor, Connecticut, shortly after I got my driver's license in the summer of 1966. My dad bought it for $695 and surprised me with it. I spent the next two days buying and installing seat belts before he would let me drive it anywhere. It cost $12 to register and title it, and $290 for a year's insurance. I really wanted a sports car, but my dad wisely insisted on something more substantial and reliable for my first car.

"My modification skills were mostly cosmetic. I pinstriped the body, blacked out the thinner bars in the grille with dad's electrical tape, replaced the full wheel covers with baby moons, and painted the valve covers and air cleaner. I added a Sun tach atop the dash because it looked cool, and not because the 283 ran out of breath at 4,200 rpm. Using the factory speaker grille in the upper middle of the rear seat, I installed a rear speaker and added a Radio Shack reverb unit for the AM radio.

"So it wasn't a sports car. I sure tried to drive it like one, but it wasn't immune to the laws of physics. The Impala soon spent some downtime and $175 at the local Amoco station getting lower profile tires, a new idler arm, and Regal Ride shocks.

"The convertible top wasn't in the best of shape, and the zipper for the rear window soon let go. That became a problem in the winter, as I would have to drive with the defroster blasting to combat the rush of cold air through the non-existent rear window. Also, I had to keep snow shoveled off the roof for fear of it caving in. Eventually, Lou Meloni put a new top and pads on it, and I learned how hard white tops were to keep clean and new looking.

"I got to drive to high school in the mid-1960s in a neat Chevy convertible, and most all of my friends drove Chevys. Stan Beauchemin had a white '64 convert, Terry Andrews had a green '59, Bill Thorpe a blue '58, Dave Boehm a black '57, and Bruce Daley's '59

A young Mike Joy is justifiably proud of his 1960 Chevy ragtop. Note license plate "MJ 77" identifying the owners initials. Mike Joy Collection

'Vette was usually seen in gray, sometimes red, primer. Gas was 33 cents per gallon, and the 283 would get around 20 miles per gallon. Life was great!

"When my first year of college was about to begin, Dad sensed (correctly) that the Impala would be a major distraction, and we sold it just after Labor Day 1967 for $475. A couple of months later, I heard the buyer had crashed in East Hartford and totaled it.

"I'd like to have one again, just for nostalgia's sake, but by today's standards, the Impala was a big-finned, good-looking parade float, dripping with chrome and stainless trim. It seemed like it was two city blocks long, and I would enjoy more horsepower and better handling. So instead, I'd prefer a slightly different horizon blue '60 Chevy convertible—a Corvette!" ■

INVOICE					MATHER MOTORS, INC.				N⁰ 2871

CUSTOMER'S COPY

MATHER MOTORS, INC.
TELEPHONE 688-3634
30 CENTRAL ST. AND 139 BROAD ST.
WINDSOR. CONNECTICUT

N⁰ 2871

May 26, 19 66

SOLD TO Mr.M. Verne Joy

ADDRESS 11 Lake View Drive   West Hartford, Conn.

SALESMAN

C 872A

NEW OR USED	MAKE	YEAR OF MODEL	IDENTIFICATION NUMBER	KEY NO.	DESCRIPTION	AMOUNT	
Used	Chevrolet	1960	01867T 215460		Blue Convertible 8 Cyl.	695	00
					Connecticut Sales Tax	24	33
					Finance Charges:		
					(If Insurance is included fill in below)		
					Insurance for Fire, Theft and dollar Deductible Collision for the benefit of the Customer for months.		
					Registration, Title, Documentary Fees	4	00
					Not Guaranteed: except		
					Total Sale	723	33
					SETTLEMENT		
					Cash on Delivery Previous Deposit	723	33
					Used Car Type I. D. No.		
	TITLE INFORMATION				No. Payments @ $ and @ $		
	Lienholder						
	Address				Total	723	33

THE ABOVE PRICES INCLUDE ANY FEDERAL EXCISE TAXES IMPOSED BY LAW

INVOICE FORM - CONN. AUTOMOTIVE TRADES ASS'N - HARTFORD   APPROVED BY MOTOR VEHICLE DEPARTMENT

A nice 1960 Impala ragtop will run a lot more than $723 these days; such was the cost of a used car back in 1966. Mike Joy Collection

GUY FIERI
1976 Datsun 280Z

In 2008, Guy Fieri competed on and won season two of The Next Food Network Star. *Today he hosts three popular shows on Food Network, including* Guy's Big Bite, *where he teaches viewers how to make creative dishes with bold flavors;* Ultimate Recipe Showdown, *where he showcases home cooks' best recipes; and* Diners, Drive-ins, and Dives, *where he travels across America to find the most unique food America has to offer. From daytime to primetime, Guy brings his unique personality to Food Network multiple times a week.*

This likeable laid-back California "guy" with his trademark bleached blond spiky hair began his love affair with food at the age of 10, selling soft pretzels from a three-wheeled bicycle cart he built with his father named The Awesome Pretzel. Through selling pretzels and washing dishes, Guy earned enough money in six years to study abroad as an exchange student in Chantilly, France. While there, he gained a true appreciation not only for international cuisine, but the culture and lifestyle associated with it.

Guy attended University of Nevada Las Vegas, where he graduated with a Bachelor's degree in Hospitality Management. He began his career with Stouffers, managing their flagship restaurant in Long Beach, California. After three years, Guy became district manager of

Fieri's loved and lost 280Z is long gone, but he seems to really enjoy the Chevelle SS convertible he currently pedals on his TV show Diners, Drive-Ins, and Dives. Guy Fieri collection

Louise's Trattoria, where he oversaw six restaurants and was in charge of recruiting and training for the growing chain.

In 1996, Guy and his business partner, Steve Gruber, embarked on a Sonoma County, California–based Italian restaurant, Johnny Garlic's. They opened their first location in Santa Rosa in the fall of 1996, a second outpost in Windsor in 1999. With the success of their first restaurant concept, they developed Tex Wasabi's, a Southern BBQ and California Sushi restaurant in 2003 in Santa Rosa, California. Guy opened a second location in Sacramento in 2007. In addition to their thriving restaurants, customers can buy fun products from t-shirts, squeeze bottles, and aprons to hats and more.

Guy has been a three-term president of the Restaurant Association of the Redwood Empire, serves on the Board of Directors for the Educational Foundation of the California Restaurant Association and most recently was grand marshall for NASCAR in Sonoma. Guy believes in using his celebrity to help others, and in the fall of 2007, the navy flew him to the Persian Gulf to entertain and cook for the troops.

I was an exchange student in France and I lived right outside of Paris. I was 16, living in France, but I wasn't allowed to drive; you can't drive in France until you're 18. I had just gotten my license in the U.S., and then I took off for France. It was terrible! Not to be able to drive! Oh man, I couldn't wait back to get to the states and be able to drive.

"When I had come back from France, I was driving my dad's pickup truck and that's how I got around. I knew I wanted to get a car but was never really comfortable with the whole idea of a car payment, so I saved and saved my money until I finally had made enough to buy the car—what I thought was going to be the car. And my buddy Johnny was selling his 280Z, and that was just way beyond the realm of what I thought I would ever get. I figured I'd just end up with an old pickup truck or something.

"So here I am, going to get this 1976 brown metallic 280Z five-speed, cherry condition, owned by an old man, and my buddy Johnny bought it. Johnny put no miles on it. Johnny only had it for six months. And there I go! This was going to be it, baby!

"Johnny was onto another car; he was always into different cars. So Johnny had the car and we started talking about a price, and I wanted to give him $3,000 and he wants $3,500 or whatever. And we go back and forth, so the deal's not going to happen.

"So my dad says, 'Did you get the car?' I said, 'No, he wants $3,500. I only have $3,000.' My dad's like, 'So, get a loan. Make payments.' I said, 'Oh, I don't want any payments. I don't want that thing over my head.'

"He's like, 'You're crazy, get the car you want.' I said, 'Nah, I can't do the payments,' and my dad had to talk me into it. I think I borrowed $500 bucks from the local bank, back then in those days. I went down to the bank and said, 'Can I borrow $500 bucks.' They said, 'Fine, sign here.' It was called the Bank of Loleta, and I went there, and Henry Weller was the bank manager, and I just turned 17. I remember everybody's name. So I bought the car and *it was my pride and joy.*

"I mean it was my everything car. I loved this car. I *still to this day* love this car. I mean, I got every car I want. But a 280Z—and every time I'll be cruising down the road, I'll see a really clean 280Z and I go, 'I gotta get that! I gotta get a 280Z!'

"So I have the car, I'm a bus boy/flambé captain up at the big restaurant in Eureka at the Red Lion. Johnny worked there, I worked there, all my buddies, we all worked there together. I drive my 280Z back and forth. I had a big piece of lambskin or lamb's wool in the back of it, and it felt nice and furry back there. Not that you can lay back there, but it is *the* bitchin' sports car. I take it to Tahoe, I go skiing with it. It's the equivalent of Michael J. Fox when he opened the garage and the black Toyota truck in *Back to the Future* was just sitting there, with his name on it, waiting for him. It's the equivalent of that to me.

"So I had the car, things are great, couldn't be happier. Another buddy had a 240Z. Everybody knew my brown 280Z. It was *immaculate*; didn't have a scratch, didn't have a dent. Perfect condition.

"I was dating Johnny's sister at the time and I was coming home from their house, driving home at night, it was late, fell asleep at the wheel, drove up onto the sidewalk, and plowed a telephone pole at 50 miles an hour and destroyed my car. I was heartbroken. Devastated.

"I broke my leg and my sternum and ribs, and got pretty banged up from the accident. I had to pay for a new telephone pole, the whole thing. This was in my hometown of Ferndale, California.

"Then I got a four-wheel-drive Blazer. I thought that would be a nice transition, 'I'll get a Blazer.' But my Blazer just never was my

280Z. So I had my Blazer, drove that a couple years, and had to get back to my 280Z. So I found another brown 280Z same year; all excited. Bought it, and it just wasn't nearly as clean or well kept or handled as my 280Z was. I had that 280Z for about a year and sold it, and that was the last 280Z.

"Everything worked on it. The antenna worked on it; everything! The first one, it was just immaculate, no scratches, no dings. It was just *the* car. It only had 50,000 miles. It still breaks my heart. I hit the telephone pole dead center. Drove the telephone pole almost up to windshield.

"It had small MOMO steering wheel, nice leather, a small sporty steering wheel. It had aftermarket mirrors on the side, louvers on the back. It was the coolest car. I *still* lament how much I miss that car. My buddy Toby and I went to Tahoe and lived in the 280Z for three days to go skiing. We didn't have enough money to get a hotel room, so we parked in the parking lot of a hotel. We parked in the hotel and snuck into a hotel room to use their shower.

"We didn't have any money, but we had enough for a lift ticket. We bought a three-day lift ticket, and we would go skiing and then hang around the casinos and stuff. And then walk back to the car, turn the car on, and sleep in our down sleeping bags. And we only had limited money, so we went to the buffet and we both made 25 prime rib sandwiches and stuffed them in our jackets, and that's what we were living off of while we were up there skiing.

"Never thought I'd have a brown car, but it was a metallic brown. I loved it! I was so upset when I wrecked it. And I wasn't drinking, it wasn't even that kind of thing. I just fell asleep at the wheel. Drove up on the sidewalk and lucky I lived, you know.

"I mean, it was a rocket ship! Nobody had a 280Z! This was 1986, it's a '76, it was 10 years old, still in its prime! I mean, it was a 280Z— waaahhhhhhhhhhhhhhhhhh [engine sound]! I do still have the Hurst shift handle that was on the car. I still have it today as the shift handle on my '71 big-block Chevelle Super Sport that was my next great car of all cars that I've had. That's all that is left! I could buy 100 280Zs for how the Chevy is built up."

That's okay, Guy, for somehow, pulling into a Midwestern diner in a 280Z just wouldn't be the same—stick with your hot rod Chevelle. ∎

—As told to K.S. Wang.

JOE MANTEGNA
1947 Buick Special

Versatile actor, writer, director, and producer Joe Mantegna was born in Chicago, Illinois, in 1947. In his younger days, he played bass for a local Chicago band before studying acting and beginning his career on stage, debuting in a performance of Hair. *He made his Broadway start in* Working, *and won a Tony award for his performance in David Mamet's* Glengarry Glen Ross. *His career spans movie and television roles across genres, from serious drama to slapstick comedy to voicing the beloved gangster Fat Tony on* The Simpsons.

"My first car was really my second car, and is a 40-year saga. Back in 1967, I was 19 and attending Morton Junior College in Cicero, Illinois. I was in a band at the time called the Apocryphals, and like any band, we needed to travel to gigs, so we needed a car, bad.

"Since the family car was on its last legs, and with a, 'Oh here, son, take this,' my father gifted me the old 1956 Chevy Bel Air. Until

Mantegna today, justifiably proud of his first car, now fully restored to its original condition. Joe Mantegna collection

In spite of years of storage and neglect, Mantegna's Buick was generally "all there" as seen here being stripped for restoration.
Joe Mantegna collection

Fortunately the car hadn't suffered any major accident damage along the way, making the restoration complex but generally straightforward, although the cost of re-chroming was no doubt considerable.
Joe Mantegna collection

then, I never had a car of my own. My family had no money, I had no money. It was the car I learned to drive in, and absconded once when I was 15 while my dad was away on business. But that old Bel Air was a real rust bucket. I remember once, my foot going through the floorboard! I would own that car for a little less than 24 hours.

"My friend spotted a 1947 Buick Special Series 41 for sale. He couldn't afford to buy it himself, so he asked if I wanted to go in halves on it with him. The car was listed for $225, and by the original owner. I thought, 'That'd be cool. Yeah, that's a cool car. This '56 Chevy is junk and the Buick looks like it was in pretty good shape.' But then my friend bails on me. He didn't have the money. I scraped up everything I had and sold the rust bucket for $75 by posting a small notice at the junior college. The Buick quickly became the band car. We were four Italian guys, we had mop-top haircuts, and we wore matching black suits, so we looked like the mob pulling up in this big black Buick.

"I drove the Buick until 1972. The Chicago winters were too tough on the old gal, so I put it in my friend's barn in La Porte, Indiana. Mostly because I didn't have the heart to give it up. It would sit there quietly for the next 20 years. My friend had a little baby at the time and I remember him telling me how the kid would play in the car. It got infested with mice and bugs, and because it was in an old rickety barn that leaked, it rusted, badly. The car became a joke. As the years went by and I began to build a life, got married, had kids, I had sort of forgotten all about it.

"Then in 1992, I got a call from my friend. He tells me he's moving and wants to know what he should do with the Buick. Now my career is going very well, I had just bought a new home out here in Los Angeles, so I figured what the hell. I tell him, 'Hey, throw it on a flat bed and send it out here.' I figured after all that history, I can't just say, 'Oh yeah, junk it.'

"But that was the tip of the iceberg. Finally, the car arrived. 'Oh my God!' I was shocked. It was unrecognizable to me. The Buick was originally black with a cloth pin-striped interior. Now it was a combination of rust, some primer grey, and well, more rust. The interior showed proof of the mouse problem in ways I won't describe. I was thrilled, however, to find memorabilia in the glove box, as well as a Midas muffler guarantee for the lifetime of the car. That week I was supposed to do an appearance on *The Tonight Show with Jay Leno*, and knowing Jay was a car buff, I brought along a picture of the car as it arrived on the flatbed. He held it up to the cameras and said, 'Call the navy, we found their anchor!' Everyone had a good laugh. But he wasn't far off. It looked like nothing could save the old Buick.

"So now what? It's here now, what do I do? I guess I could chalk it up as a loss, but then I thought, this is my first car. I have all these memories in this car, and it was manufactured the same year I was born. Tossing this car away would be the equivalent of somebody tossing me away! I decided I was going to do right by it. That started a journey of restoring the old Buick that would last 12 years.

"I had joined the Buick Club of America in 1967. After the car was put in mothballs, I let the membership expire. I called to reactivate my membership and when they looked me up, they said, 'Wow, you're one of the first 5,000!' I was like royalty to them. The club now has over 40,000 members. Through the club, I found a guy named Les Peoples in Van Nuys, California. He was an expert on restoring old Buicks.

"Now, living in California, the idea of driving around in a big black car with this kind of itchy upholstery wasn't very appealing. My wife said, 'Make it a California car; make it the car that you would want to drive here today.' She was right. After years of a painstaking frame-off restoration, searching the world for parts, rebuilding everything from the engine to the radio, even buying a second Buick to cannibalize, and an amount of money I don't dare reveal just on the off chance my wife reads this, it was finally done!

"The car now has a chocolate and cream leather interior that is only surpassed in beauty by the camel beige exterior. It looks like a California '47 Buick now, complete with California plates. If the Buick could talk, I'm sure it would say it's right at home here in sunny Los Angeles. No snow, no hail, no salty roads filled with slush and no more freezing mornings trying to coax her to start.

"Not far from me is George Barris' studio; a man I idolized growing up. If you were a kid in the early '60s, especially being from a place like Chicago as I was, he was this mysterious guy out in California who took car customizing to a level I had never known. And what's more, he was one of us—he was from Chicago! There were other customizers at the time—Tony Nancy and Ed 'Big Daddy'

Joe's band poses in front of the Buick in the late 1960s; Joe Mantegna at left front. Joe Mantegna collection

Roth—but to me, George Barris was the king. Now I'm very proud to call him a friend, and was equally flattered when he invited me to speak at a ceremony when the city of Los Angeles renamed an intersection George Barris Square.

"Down the street from George is a historic Bob's Big Boy. Built in 1949, it still has carhop service on weekends. Every Friday afternoon, guys with old cars in different states of restoration start showing up. It's like stepping into a time machine. They dote over their cars, and I'm sure they picture themselves at 17 with slicked back hair and a pack of Lucky Strikes rolled under one sleeve of their t-shirt. I go there to look at the cars and talk with guys who share the passion.

"Les Peoples passed away recently. He was a good man and knew his craft well. My Buick was one of his last. I drive it to car shows now and then. I've won a couple of awards. But often I just cruise around, sometimes to work or just to remind myself how much I love this car. It still has that signature Buick ride, like you're floating on wheels made of clouds. As you can imagine, I get a lot of looks, a lot of honks, and a lot of thumbs up. I suppose some are for me, and in a way some are for Les, but mostly they're for the Buick, and how it reminds people of something they will always remember fondly—their youth."

Mantegna's Buick remains in excellent condition, although he has no plans to put his band back together and hit the road any time soon. ■

—As told to K.S. Wang.

Johnny Carson

1939 CHRYSLER ROYAL

Born in 1925 in Corning, Iowa, Johnny Carson established what has ultimately become the standard format for television chat shows and came to be considered "the king of late night television. Following high school and service in the Navy during World War II, Carson enrolled at the University of Nebraska where he participated in student theater and began working for a radio station in Lincoln. His radio work led to a Sunday afternoon comedy show, which led to a job writing for comedian Red Skelton. He was given his own short-lived variety show, and then moved to New York City and became host of the game show Who Do You Trust?. Carson replaced Jack Parr as host of The Tonight Show, going on to host for three decades prior to handing the show off to Jay Leno.

> ## *"The car doesn't have quite the pick-up it used to, but then neither do I."*

"My first car was a green 1939 Chrysler Royal. It was my father's car, so it was free. I got it when I was a junior at Norfolk High School in Nebraska.

"The most memorable experience I had in the car was losing my virginity. As in all small towns in those days, there were 'nice girls,' girls that you married, and girls that you did not. Well, in Norfolk, there was this girl, I'll call her Francine, and Francine, well, 'put out'—at least that was the story that was going around. When I finally got up enough nerve to ask her out and she said yes, you can imagine my excitement—Mount Vesuvius! However, I had one problem to overcome: protection. I went up to the drugstore counter, and the druggist hollers, 'Well, John, what can I do for you?' Luckily, he saw that I had Francine waiting in the car and knowingly handed over the goods. I remember I had, as we used to put it, a 'swell' time.

"I still have the car. A steelworker in Norfolk restored it beautifully and NBC gave it to me as a birthday present. The car doesn't have quite the pick-up it used to, but then neither do I." ∎

Carson's much-loved Chrysler lives at the Imperial Palace Auto Collection in Las Vegas, and remains in clean, original condition. Kirk Gerbracht photo

STEVE MCQUEEN
MG TC

As an actor and cult hero of intergalactic proportion, Steve McQueen needs no introduction here or anywhere else. From his first bits on Broadway in the 1950s to his well-earned place as one of the world's most popular actors, McQueen's star power lived large. McQueen was once nominated for a Best Acting Oscar, although didn't win. An avid and capable automobile racer, he placed second, teamed with professional road racer Peter Revson, at the 12 Hours of Sebring in 1970, driving a Porsche 908 Spyder with his foot in a cast due to injuries received in a motorcycle accident that took place just a few weeks prior to the Florida race. Cars, motorcycles, and racing often factored into McQueen's films, with him, more often than not, at the wheel or the handlebars when the cameras were rolling. Even now, more than 25 years after his untimely passing on November 7, 1980, his legend is intact, his legacy as relevant as ever. But beyond his status on stage and screen, Steve McQueen was a certifiable motorhead.

He helped build a hot rod before he could legally drive. In the service, he hopped up a tank's engine in the hopes of getting it to go faster. As a young acting student, he rode motorcycles through Greenwich Village. In 1970, he nearly won the 12 Hours of Sebring in a Porsche 908. He raced buggies in Baja, rode motorcycles all over the world, and built entire movies around his love of automobiles and motorsport. McQueen would street race his rare Jaguar XK-SS through the Hollywood Hills at night, then pack a pickup full of pals and dirt bikes, and spend the next day busting trails through the California desert. He entered motorcycle races under the pseudonym "Henry Mushman" so that spectators and the other competitors wouldn't treat him differently than anyone else. Pinstriping pioneer Von Dutch, auto upholstery legend Tony Nancy, motorcycle champion Malcolm Smith, and dirt bike racer/stuntman Bud Ekins were among his inner circle.

Many enthusiasts caught the sports car bug at the wheel of an MG TC, including McQueen during his early days as a stage actor in New York. *Chad McQueen Collection*

"He raced buggies in Baja, rode motorcycles all over the world, and built entire movies around his love of automobiles and motorsport."

"We had this old tank," he said, "and I thought it could be souped up. So a couple of guys and me, we really worked it over, porting and milling the heads, fooling around with the timing and carburetion. Well, on the day we finished, we took it out for a timed run. And the laugh was on us; it didn't go any faster."

As his status as an actor grew, so did the influence he had over the content of his films. He often wove cars and motorcycles into those plotlines—with him at the wheel or gripping the handlebars, of course. In the case of 1971's Le Mans, racing was the film's reason for being, so hungry was McQueen to make the most realistic motorsport movie ever.

At 12, he helped an older pal assemble a hot rod. "It had an Edelbrock manifold" on its compact Ford V8-60 flathead V-8 engine, and "could accelerate with a J-2 Allard, which was *the* going sports car around this time. Our rod didn't handle for beans, but when the engine stayed together that machine had *stark* acceleration."

McQueen's formative years were tough, to say the least. He never went to school beyond the ninth grade, and lived for a while at the Boys Republic reform school in Chino, California. He has his challenges there too, although always spoke fondly of this institution, and supported it generously throughout his adult life.

At the age of 17, he joined the Marine Corps, and it was there he again exhibited his love of things mechanical. He was assigned to the tank corps. "We had this old tank," he said, "and I thought it could be souped up. So a couple of guys and me, we really worked it over, porting and milling the heads, fooling around with the timing and carburetion. Well, on the day we finished, we took it out for a timed run. And the laugh was on us; it didn't go *any* faster."

After his three-year stint in the service and an honorable discharge, McQueen moved to New York. It was there that he acquired the first motorized thing he could call his own, an Indian motorcycle with a sidecar. It was the first of hundreds of street and racing motorcycles he would own, but the automobile that Steve McQueen loved first was the sports car that America loved first as well: an MG TC, which he bought in 1952.

Not long after arriving in The Big Apple, he began studying acting. Soon, he was performing in small, off-Broadway plays, with varying levels of success. A traveling production of *Time Out for Ginger* brought him to Columbus, Ohio, where he found the MG. Between his pay and poker winnings, McQueen saved up $450. But the owner was asking $750. "I put down $450, and I told the owner I'd send more money from each overnight stop we made. Which I did. It was finally delivered to me in Chicago. That's when I asked for a raise and got booted out of the play. So, I jumped into my MG and drove it all the way back to New York."

The fun but fragile sports car wasn't the ideal machine for the mean streets of Manhattan. "I sold it after three axles broke" he said, "and the spokes kept shredding out of those wire wheels. I decided to stick with cycles for a while." ■

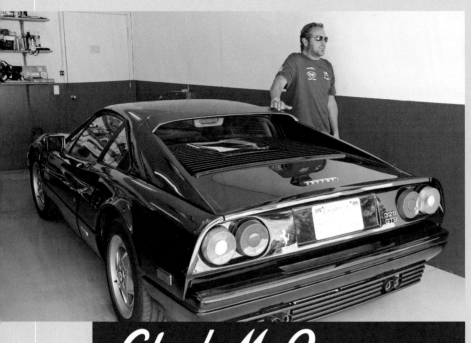

Chad McQueen

1949 CHEVROLET PICKUP

Chad McQueen is the only son of legendary actor/racer Steve McQueen and actress/dancer/singer Neile Adams McQueen. Chad has worked as a film actor for some time, appearing as Dutch in The Karate Kid and The Karate Kid Part II, and many other roles, including a role in the 1995 film New York Cop with Mira Sorvino, and the lead in the action film Red Line. He has also worked as a producer, winning a Telly Award for his documentary Filming at Speed. He has appeared on numerous television programs related to motorsports, including Hot Rod TV and Celebrity Rides. He was also a capable road racer in his own right, having competed in the Baja 1,000 off-road race, earning an SCCA national driving championship, and also raced in the Grand-American road racing series top Daytona Prototype category.

Clearly no Chevy pickup, McQueen and his Ferrari 328/GTB.
Author photo

"My five-window cab Chevy truck had a straight six-cylinder engine and a 'three on the tree' manual transmission. I worked over a year at a gas station to save the money to buy it from my dad. I paid about $2,200 for it. I think he overcharged me. That was about 1976. It was British Racing Green with a dark brown interior and a big bench seat. I loved that thing and never had any trouble with it, except that it threw a fan belt now and again, so I always carried an extra belt with me.

"I kept the truck all these years and was having it fully restored, and just a few years back, someone broke into the shop where it was being worked on and stole it. I used to go everywhere in that thing; me and my buddies or girls or whomever. I never really went far, so it spent most of its time around our Malibu home. People always reacted positively to that truck; it looked so good in that shiny dark green. I used to get so many thumbs up in that thing, and I'm really sad that it's gone."

McQueen still loves cars, owning several Porsches that belonged to his late father, plus the first 2008 Bullitt edition Mustang produced, and an all-black Ferrari 328GTB. ∎

Chad McQueen remains a consummate car, motorcycle, and motorsport enthusiast, seen here with his 1968 "Bullitt" Mustang replica, in tribute to one of his father's most famous and enduring movie cars. Author photo

PAUL NEWMAN
1929 Ford Model A

Paul Newman's legendary life as an actor, director, and world class philanthropist is well known. Less known to many was his passion for motorsport, not only as a serious and capable sports car racer, but also as an Indy car racing team co-owner. Newman's racing flame was lighted once and for all when he starred in Winning, *filmed in 1968, which was set around the life and times of a journeyman racing driver who overcame tough odds to win the Indianapolis 500. His co-stars were real life wife Joanne Woodward and Robert Wagner, the latter playing his oft-times competitor and teammate. Newman earned his Sports Car Club of America racing license in 1972, and joined forces with Connecticut Datsun dealer, racer, and race team owner Bob Sharp. Newman won numerous SCCA national titles, several Trans-Am races, and even competed at the 24 Hours of Le Mans in 1979. His last SCCA win came in 2007 at the age of 82, at the wheel of a 700-horsepower GT1-class Corvette. Yet his first car was a humble Ford Model A.*

Paul Newman wasn't born a car guy. "It all came to me very late in life," he told *Motor Trend* magazine in a 1970 interview. "I guess I've been interested in sports cars and bikes for about 10 or 12 years, but it's always been kind of Mickey Mouse with me."

Paul Leonard Newman was born January 26, 1925, in Shaker Heights, Ohio. Like so many young actors in the postwar era, he moved to New York to study and pursue his craft. In the early 1950s, he appeared in numerous on- and off-Broadway productions. He made his television debut in 1952 in a futuristic, sci-fi television show called *Tales of Tomorrow*, and his first movie role came along two years later in a romance/drama titled *The Silver Chalice*.

Newman's first car was a 1929 Ford Model A. It was followed by a 1937 Packard, for which he paid $150 sometime in the late 1940s. He was married to his first wife, Jackie Witte, still living in Ohio, and renting a two-bedroom apartment for the princely sum of $10 per month. After moving to New York, he bought his first of many

Actor, auto racing enthusiast, and racing team owner Paul
Newman (left) stands talking to another man in an auto garage,
Florida, 1967. Newman was a big fan of VWs, although it is
not known if the Beetle to Newman's right belonged to him.
Photo by Mark Kauffman/Time & Life Pictures/Getty Images

"Newman's first car was a 1929
Ford Model A. It was followed by
a 1937 Packard, for which he paid
$150 sometime in the late 1940s."

Volkswagens in 1953. It remained factory stock for the next eight years or so, but then he got the notion to hop it up a bit. He had by then relocated his primary residence to Connecticut, with second wife, Joanne Woodward, and their growing family. The VW was still serving faithfully, but Newman had grown tired of all the gear shifting required during his commute. It was then that his enthusiasm for high-performance cars began to manifest itself.

"I was complaining to my mechanic about driving the VW back and forth to the theater in New York and my home in Connecticut," he told *Motor Trend*. "He said 'Why don't you dump a Porsche engine in it, and you'll still retain your back seat but have all the power you need.' So we dropped in a stock Porsche engine, installed sway bars, Konis [shock absorbers], and Dunlop Super Sports [tires]. The car handled so well that we put in a Porsche Super 90 engine, and then put Porsche brakes up front. Later we bored out the Super 90 to 1,800cc and put a hot cam in it. It was a neat little bomb." ∎

"The VW was still serving faithfully, but Newman had grown tired of all the gear shifting required during his commute. It was then that his enthusiasm for high-performance cars began to manifest itself."

EDWARD HERRMANN
1956 Austin-Healey 100-6

Edward Herrmann attended the London Academy of Music and Dramatic Arts on a Fulbright scholarship. His distinguished stage, theatrical, and television career has garnered him Emmy and Tony awards, plus numerous nominations. Herrmann won his Tony Award for Mrs. Warren's Profession *in 1976, the same year that Kelly Bishop, his co-star on* Gilmore Girls, *snagged her Tony for* A Chorus Line. *He has as played FDR three times: in the 1976 TV-movie* Eleanor and Franklin, *the 1977 sequel* Eleanor and Franklin: The White House Years, *and in the 1982 movie musical* Annie.

"I bought the Healey in California for $2,300. It wasn't in really bad shape, it was just a mess. It needed lots of cosmetics. It was my first experience with all the alarms and diversions of auto restoration, and a shop that did reasonably good work but was full of lies, prevarications, and delays and all that.

"When the car was refinished, in British Racing Green, with the proper painted wire wheels, I learned all about the trials running an old English sports car in often-hot Southern California. The

Herrmann's Auburn crosses the awards ramp at Pebble Beach.
Pebble Beach Concours d'Elegance

STARS OF STAGE, SCREEN, AND SOUND

137

Herrmann in one of his best known automotive roles, as master of ceremonies at the Pebble Beach Concours d'Elegance. Pebble Beach Concours d'Elegance

Healey had great legroom, but my legs just broiled in that long footwell because that six-cylinder engine threw off so much heat. I would burn my foot on the metal accelerator pedal. But I loved it; it was terrific. So I'd have to change feet about every 50 miles or so. I would lose about 10 pounds every time I drove it for a day. It was the perfect car for 40 degree days with the top down. After I spent about $5,000 on new paint, tires, redoing the engine, and such, I had a wonderful car.

"I would leave it in a garage in California, and then head back to New York to work. Then when a job or audition in California came up, I'd go to get the car, and of course the tires would be flat and the battery dead. Then I'd spruce it up and get it going again. It actually became a little too much to handle, having to do that every time I needed to get around Hollywood. I don't remember any specific road trip stories. Most often, I needed it to get me to an audition. When I arrived in L.A., I'd always wonder if it would start or have a flat tire, and I usually showed up to the meeting tired and drenched in sweat

True Brit. Herrmann's much beloved, navy blue Aston Martin. Pebble Beach Concours d'Elegance

(especially in summer). Just the usual 'old British car syndrome,' although the electrics were pretty sound. It was my L.A. car, and I drove it all over the basin or out to Malibu. No matter, I just loved that car. I don't remember to whom or exactly when I sold it—I think I got about $5,000 or $6,000 for it.

"After a while when my career got going, I started doing commercials for Dodge, and then had a more steady income, which allowed me to play a bit with cars instead of just rely on them for transportation. Then, out of Hemmings, I bought a '38 Packard Six convertible. The car was a real disaster; an idiotic buy on my part. All of these things are lessons along the old car highway. It cost me, oh, I can't remember how much to redo it. We had to buy another car and strip it for parts. The guy who did for me was a good guy, but also on a learning curve. In spite of all the 'lessons,' it really came out beautiful."

Herrmann knows his stuff and remains a committed automobile enthusiast, owning several interesting vintage cars, and serves as master of ceremonies at the Pebble Beach Concours d'Elegance. ∎

Dan Ackroyd

1939 DODGE SEDAN

Its only appropriate that Ackroyd's first car was a Dodge, since one of his most enduring film roles is as Elwood Blues, piloting a Dodge ex-police cruiser in the "Blues Brothers" with pal John Belushi. David Hartley/Rex USA

Actor and comedian Dan Ackroyd was one of the original Not Ready for Prime Time Players on Saturday Night Live. *An avid automobile and motorcycle enthusiast, one of Ackroyd's best known automotive relative movie lines was delivered when playing character Elwood Blues in the movie* The Blues Brothers, *filmed in partnership with his long time friend, the late John Belushi. As the two brothers debated as to if a newly acquired former police cruiser would be adequate transport, Ackroyd (Elwood) stoically said to Belushi (Joliet Jake),* "It's got a cop motor, a 440-cubic-inch plant, it's got cop tires, cop suspension, cop shocks. It's a model made before catalytic converters so it'll run good on regular gas. What do you say, is it the new Bluesmobile or what?"

"It was a 1939 Dodge flathead six, four-door sedan, with a three-speed shift on the column. It had a black paint job that was done with a broom so that the marks, the brushstrokes, were quite evident on the sides; there were actual ridges of paint on the car. And that particular model had the suicide doors. You know, the back doors that opened out.

"My father bought it for $125. I was the lucky fifth owner of the vehicle. My dad installed a cassette tape player in the dashboard and provided tapes by Benny Goodman, Jack Hilton, Freddy Gardner, Ray Noble—all the old 1940s swing bands. We'd drive in the car and play the old music, and it would really take us back.

"My friends and I went to college and went to concerts in it, and we dressed for the car—the double-breasted suit with the pleated pants, and the slicked-down hair. We tried to look as much as possible like soldiers from the Canadian army in 1939 having a civilian night out.

"In the wintertime when it snowed, I used the old car to drag my friends behind me. They would put on heavy boots, hook on to the back bumper, and do what in Canada was called 'bunking.' I'd drag the boys behind the old Dodge—it was just like skiing with a car pulling you. You just had to watch out for manhole covers.

"Somewhere, there's a beautiful shot of me and a friend sitting on the hood of this car. We look like two old crows sitting out in a field. Ken Danby, a Canadian realist painter, has a painting called 'From the Summer of '38;' a beautiful picture, with what looks like my Dodge sitting in a field. That's exactly what happened to my first car: It ended up just like the one in that painting." ∎

ERIC BANA
1974 Australian Ford Falcon XB Coupe

Eric Bana was born Eric Banadinovich in Melbourne, Victoria, Australia. He is the younger of two brothers. His father, named Ivan Banadinovich, came from Zagreb, Croatia, and worked as a manager for Caterpillar Inc. His mother, named Eleanor Banadinovich, came from a German family and was a hairdresser.

Young Bana grew up in suburban Melbourne. He was popular among his schoolmates for his talent of making comic impressions of his teachers. At that time, he was fond of Mel Gibson in Mad Max, *and also decided to become an actor. He moved to Sydney and worked odd jobs to support himself. In 1991, he began a career as a stand-up comedian, while working as a barman at Melbourne's Castle Hotel. He made his film debut in* The Castle *in a supporting comic role. That same year, he was cast to portray Mark "Chopper" Read, the notorious Australian underworld figure. Then he co-starred in* Black Hawk Down, *then* Hulk. *In 2005, Bana co-starred with Daniel Craig and Geoffrey Rush in the political drama* Munich, *directed by Steven Spielberg.*

He currently resides in Melbourne with his wife and their two children. Bana produced and directed a feature film in 2009 about his beloved Falcon XB, co-starring Jay Leno, Jeremy Clarkson, and "Dr. Phil" Walters, entitled Love the Beast.

"I grew up in suburban Melbourne surrounded by big cars with big engines. And I always loved this XB coupe body style; there's a bit of American Mustang and Torino in it, but it's quite a bit more muscular, really, and better proportioned, I feel, especially in the Coke-bottle shape of the rear bodywork.

"A pair of XBs finished 1-2 at Bathurst [Australia's biggest motor race] in 1977, which was a big deal, and I was hooked for good. Just had to have one. I was already well determined to have a Falcon coupe by the time Mel Gibson drove a black, heavily modified version [called the Interceptor] of a similar car in the original *Mad Max*, a film that melded the two things I love most: hot cars and cinema.

Humble beginnings. A teenaged Bana with his Falcon, as acquired, still running tired white paint and a six-cylinder engine. Eric Bana collection

Bana today, and his much modified, race-restored Falcon, prior to meeting up with a tree on the Targa Tasmanian open road race. Eric Bana collection

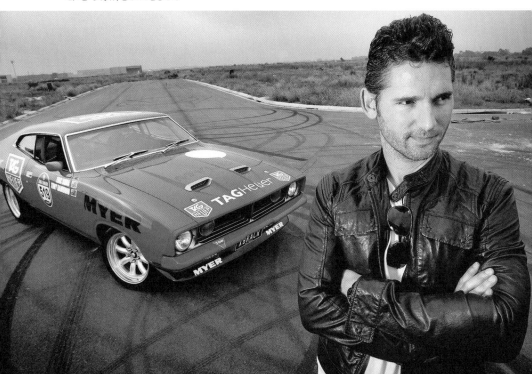

"Mine was a somewhat sad piece when I found it, and I just bought it prior to turning 16. It was white, all there, but very rough around the edges. I paid the U.S. equivalent of about $800 for it, and my friends and I worked on it incessantly. I always wanted to be a racing driver, and then we decided to prepare the Falcon for a run in the Targa Tasmania open road rally in 1996. It's a mad event, run on closed public roads, through the suburbs and the mountains. It was still powered by its original inline six-cylinder engine, and we prepped it the best we could finishing an amazing third place in its class.

"Several years later I decided to restore it, but what started out as a strip down for paint became something else entirely. The job ended up encompassing a complete nut and bolt rebuild, plus the conversion to a pretty serious road race car that we would run in the vintage division of the Targa Tasmania open road rally. The six came out, and in went a 600-horsepower Ford Racing Windsor V-8. We did a full roll cage and a pretty race-inspired suspension, although we kept the leaf springs in the back. And we painted the whole thing a brilliant shade of red.

"Things were going well in the 2007 Targa Tas. We were running a particularly difficult stage, when I lost the car and went nose-first into a tree, hard. Neither I nor my co-driver was hurt, but I was heartbroken at what I'd done to the car, and especially for all the hard work by so many people that went into the effort. I didn't know how bad it was until later when were tearing the car down to begin assessing the repair job we were to be faced with.

"This car has been a campfire for my friends and family to gather around, literally and figuratively. It was a physical reason to get together and gather for us. And it has remained that, as a constant for so many of us. Like the campfire, it has always kept burning, and remains the physical manifestation of something we all gather around. As of now, the body and chassis has been rebuilt, and is ready for paint. I've toned it down just a bit to make it a little easier to drive on the street, and I suspect its racing days are at an end. But I'll never sell it. It's been with me too long and is too much a part of me now. Life has taken me on a surreal and unexpected journey, but two things have remained constant—my mates and my beast." ∎

GREGG ALLMAN

1934 Chevrolet five-window coupe

Gregg Allman, born in Nashville in 1947, is a rock and roll and blues guitarist and keyboardist who, with his brother Duane, formed the Allman Brothers band. Allman also enjoys riding motorcycles. In spite of Duane's passing, Gregg continues to tour with the rest of the band, and remains a popular performer the world over.

"I started playing when I was 9, got my first guitar when I was 10, and I didn't think about anything but playing and getting a ride. I've always *loved* automobiles and bikes. I've just always loved them. Whether I was legal or not, just trying to get something I could call 'my ride.' And I had two or three of them even before I was supposed to have them.

Allman today, remembering all the blood, sweat, tears, and hard work he put into his 1934 Chevy. *Gregg Allman*

"It was the summer between my sophomore year and junior year in high school. I had a learner's permit and I rented this old garage that was just, oh God, it was dark and dank. I rode back the last time I was home, and damn if the old garage still ain't there. It's still there.

"I had more pride in and I suffered more and I put more back-breaking work in my 1934 Chevy five-window coupe, the same kind of car as the ZZ Top car. At that time you could get a learner's permit at age 14, but it had to be daytime and you had to have a licensed driver riding with you to drive legally. And that was slim to none.

"I bought it for $60 from this old surfer in Daytona Beach; that's where I grew up. He was drunk and I think he was on the run from the law; that's why I got it so cheap. It really was. It was worth a lot, a lot more than that, even back then. I'd been seeing him driving it around and so I knew it ran already. I didn't buy a pig in a poke just because it looked good. No, no, no, no, no. And it had great traction—I mean that thing would bark, oh, look out! There was no weight to it at all. It was like an outboard motor on a plank. I approached him one day to buy it and he said, 'Funny you should ask!'

"The motor mounts would actually allow you to fit in a 1956 Starfire Oldsmobile small-block V-8. And those engines, some of them came out with three deuces on them. The big ones did—that was a 98. My Chevy had a Rocket 88 engine in it.

"It was grey, like primer grey, flat grey. He tried to cut a sunroof in it. It looked like it was cut right. It looked like it was factory cut, the top, and it looked like they tried to cover it with some kind of canvas material to have a moonroof.

"It looked so fine. One thing he had done to it, he put heavy duty shocks on it because there's a very short wheelbase. You sat right on the floor, and they were suicide doors; the doors were hinged at the rear and opened front ways. It didn't open the way most car doors open. There was just one on each side, and it was a two-seater of course. And it had cheater slicks on the back of it, and they were *real* big—that's the slicks—but it has tread on it, and it had regular car tires on the front, which gave it that shape of kind of a pointed deal. There were smaller wheels in the front and larger wheels in the back, yet it sat level. It was really done nicely. It had a B&M hydrostick, that means you just switch it from automatic over to four-speed.

Allman's mom boards his chopper while the rocker hangs on to Mom's puppy. Gregg Allman

"Also it had a truck clutch in it. I'm not sure what size that was. But it was hard to push in, let me tell ya. It would leap, because with that plywood floorboard, there was no bend in the floor board. I mean, our floorboard goes up, then you got the pedals. When you're driving the stick you adjust your clutch down a little bit low, so you let the clutch all the way out without moving your heel. It's just the front part of your foot comes up and you're all the way out, that's the way all my cars are. Damn, having the thing engage when you're all the way out, that's crazy, because if you're in traffic, who wants to have that thing jerking and all that. So I had it adjusted down like that with a little help from my friends.

"As far as taking pictures of it, that's something that you just didn't think of back then. You didn't carry around a telephone and a camera with you, like people do now. Ah, times have changed. They used to wave cigarette lighters at concerts, now they wave cell phones. From the stage, looking out, you see this sea of cell phones. You look out at 25,000 people and you see all of them with a cell phone waving it and I wonder what the cell phones are on. Are they recording?

"Just when I got it where I really, really dig it and got it cranked up and got the wiring, it was like spaghetti under the dash and I had to tear it all out and go, one to one, one to one, one to one—it was all done by colors back then. I had a lot of help on that. Just as that happened, somebody ratted on me. They didn't really rat on me. An old man came down to collect for his garage and my mother was like, 'What garage?' About time I walked up, I said, 'What are you doing here?' She didn't know I had a car, she didn't know I had a garage, she didn't know nothin' about nothin'! When she saw the damn thing, it was just deathtrap in her eyes. She said 'Sell it, sell it! Or I'll give it away!' I sold the damn thing. I sold it in a matter of hours after that. I had the car about four and a half weeks; long enough to really fall in love with it.

"I took quite a few putts on it. I took it on the beach. That's back when you didn't have to pay to get on the beach and it was a good place to go down and drive. At that particular time, which would have been about 1963, 1964—about the time Mustang first came out—you didn't necessarily have to have a current license tag. To get a tag for it, I would have had to take a licensed driver down there with me, and of course that driver would have held some responsibility, so I couldn't just get an older friend of mine to just do it because they didn't get involved. And momma—can't get her to do it because then she'll find out about the car. And I knew exactly what her reaction would be, and that would be, 'Sell it, sell it!' So it was a bit of a paradox, I swear. It was an experience though, and that was the good part about it.

"I picked up a lot of nice-looking girls in it. It was back during that summer that you finally realized that girls are not soft boys. Well, no, I had noticed before that, but I now had a wagon to haul 'em around in, if you know what I mean. I played at the pier, as a matter of fact. I set out one night to drive the damn thing up to the pier so the ladies walking out onto the pier, going to the Ocean Pier Casino, [which] was the name of the place that we played in. It was called the House Rockers and the Un-Tils, the band was. There wasn't a casino. It was just called that.

"I sold it to this rich kid down the street who was green with envy every time we'd go up and worked on it. He'd wanna watch; he'd wanna watch. I said, 'Man, not only do you get to watch, you can own for just a mere $120! He says, 'But that's twice what you paid for it, man!' I said, 'But look at all the time and labor and money I had put into it.' He forked over $120 and it was his. Yep.

"I hated seeing it go away. Oh, it was neat; it was neat. It was a street rod, face it. And I'll tell ya, I've wanted one ever since then and before it's all over with, *I will have one*." ■

—As told to K.S. Wang.

MATT SCANNELL
1992 Ford Explorer

Matt Scannell, lead singer and songwriter of the band Vertical Horizon, has written seven hit singles. His songs have been featured in the films Bruce Almighty, Driven, *and the television shows,* Friends *and* Smallville.

Matt and his band tour five months out of the year in a Prevost bus, in which he is happy to leave the driving to someone else. When he's back home in Los Angeles, Matt rolls in his BMW M5. The raucous twisty thread of road that runs atop the Hollywood Hills—Mulholland Drive—is one element of his commute to his songwriting studio in storied Laurel Canyon. "For me, being home is all about where I'm going to drive," he says. "Luckily, my everyday commute is filled with tight turns, elevation changes, and off-camber glories."

"The year was 1992 and I was 21. I was serious about making a go of it and getting Vertical Horizon established. I was graduating from Georgetown, and we decided the best way to get a following would be to tour the country. I needed a vehicle that could carry a lot of gear—our PA system, several guitars, T-shirts, CDs, and our luggage. This was going to be our first 'tour bus.'

"It's funny because as far back as I can remember, I've been obsessed with sports cars. As a kid I dreamt of my parents owning them and of me driving them. So how ironic that when it came to choosing my first vehicle, it was a Ford Explorer. It was dark green with a tan interior and it cost $19,000. My parents bought it for me as a graduation gift from Harr Ford in Worchester, Massachusetts. They knew I'd be traveling all of the country and they wanted me to be in something new and reliable. I just wanted to make sure it wasn't the Eddie Bauer edition, because that would be so lame and embarrassing with all those logos everywhere.

"When I was growing up, all through the 1980s, I subscribed to *Road & Track*, *Car and Driver*, and *Motor Trend*, and when *Automobile* came out, I subscribed to that magazine too—I read them all voraciously. I guess it was in my genes to love racy cars because I came

Some friends chide Scannell about his choosing an Explorer as his first car, but he doesn't regret the pick at all, needing the room for his friends, bandmates, and musical equipment. *Bobby Bank/WireImage/Getty Images*

home from the hospital on the backseat shelf of my dad's butter-scotch-colored Porsche 912. He also had a chocolate brown Triumph TR6 and a British Racing Green Austin-Healey. My dad loves cars to this day.

"When I was in my mid-teens, I hatched a plot to buy a Porsche 959. I thought that if I could get a bit of money from every member of my family, kind of like putting together a timeshare, that we could flip it and make a huge profit. It was so funny, I was 16 or so, and here I was spearheading this effort to invest in collectible cars. Of course, my plan wasn't greeted with enthusiasm by my elders and we never did buy the 959. I had big ideas back then. Still do.

"Anyway, that Explorer turned out to be a great choice. It wasn't the kind of thing that set my pulse racing, but I was on the road 200 nights per year and my Explorer became my home. It was dependable and functional, and it allowed me to chase my dream of becoming a musician. Yes, I'm passionate about sports cars, but the Explorer taught me about utility and functionality and it helped me get my work done.

"From 1992 to 1997, I was on the road all the time: Chicago, Colorado, Texas, up and down the East Coast a thousand times. The Explorer's four-wheel drive was incredible. The snow would be coming down, and we'd have a gig in Tennessee, and we'd make it! It was a never-say-die car. It served me well and was such a workhorse, so faithful and kind to me. And yet, I never wanted to go out and *wash* it, you know? All that passion I have about cars was put on pause. The visceral thrill I have in driving, that I experience now, well, it wasn't in the vocabulary back then. There was nothing exciting about it—it wasn't a 911 or a Countach…

"I don't think I could get another Explorer today. I spent so much time in it—with the fun side of me shut down for so long—the guy who loves sports cars and gorgeous cars, I just can't go back. The genie is out of the bottle and I want my cars to be a bit *more*. So today, I have a BMW M5, which is guess is the perfect balance between an Explorer and a 911 because I can fit my Marshall 4x12—a big speaker cabinet—in the car along with five of my guitars and a pedalboard, head off to a gig or the studio and enjoy the drive along the way.

"It's got a V-10, 507-horsepower engine, and it really is practical. It satisfies my need to haul gear and my obsession with sports cars. Yes, I love this thing—it's crazy how much—but I'll always have affection for that reliable Explorer and how it helped me launch my career."

Scannel is often chided about choosing something so pedestrian as an Explorer as his first car, but defends the choice as being practical and logical for hauling his friends and band gear. ■

—AS TOLD TO TARA WEINGARTEN

OFFICIAL PACE CAR

Morgan Freeman
1952 FORD CONVERTIBLE

The original *Easy Reader* on television's Electric Company, *Morgan Freeman went on to become an Academy Award nominee for* Street Smart, The Shawshank Redemption, Driving Miss Daisy, *and* Invictus. *He won an Academy Award for his role in Clint Eastwood's* Million Dollar Baby.

Freeman, still showing his enthusiasm for automobiles, at the wheel of the Corvette Pace Car prior to the start of the 1994 Indianapolis 500. AP Photo/Tom Strattman

> ## "Life changed.
> ## It was like day and night.
> ## Without a car, I couldn't get a date.
> ## Then when I got a car,
> ## I turned 'em down."

"Like all kids in high school, I desperately wanted a car but I didn't need one. I grew up in Mississippi. In a small town, you walk everywhere you want to go; you get there in jig time. You get used to that. Then as a teenager, I had a bicycle. Then I was gone—I was in the service. A lot of guys in the service had cars and, of course, I always befriended somebody who had a car.

"I had been working for about eight months at the Los Angeles City College for $60 a week. Gross. I saw this car in a lot for $500. It was a 1952 white Ford convertible. I managed to get a down payment and I bought it, and there I was in wheels. Life changed. It was like day and night. Without a car, I couldn't get a date. Then when I got a car, I turned 'em down.

"I remember once I was going out with some friends. We were going to the Moulin Rouge on Sunset. I had too much to drink, it was my car, and I was driving. I thought, 'I'm fine, I'm just terrific, I can do this.' I was so sure of myself, so positive that I had everything under control. Well, I got into the parking lot at the Moulin Rouge and ran right into the side of a bus with my car. I didn't damage the car. It was a 1952 car, and they made 'em out of good stuff then. But I didn't drink and drive anymore after that." ■

MIKE LOVE
1949 Chevrolet

Mike Love formed the Beach Boys along with his cousins Brian, Carl, and Dennis Wilson, and their friend Al Jardine. Although he played the saxophone in the early days, Mike Love was mainly the co-lead singer, along with Brian Wilson. Love sang the lead vocal on many of the Beach Boys' biggest hits, including "Surfin' Safari," "Surfin' USA," "Little Deuce Coupe," "Be True to Your School," "Fun, Fun, Fun," "Little Saint Nick," "I Get Around," "When I Grow Up (To Be a Man)," and "California Girls." His lead vocal roles later diminished as other members' voices took center stage He is also known for his bass vocals, such as the vocal break in "I Can Hear Music" and the bass line in "Good Vibrations." Love also wrote or co-wrote lyrics to many of the Beach Boys songs, mostly with the themes of surfing, cars, or love, but also memorable ballads such as "The Warmth of the Sun." Throughout his career he continues to co-write numerous songs, and has written several songs on his own.

A definitely beachy, if somewhat serious looking, Mike Love and his MG, the first of many great British cars in his stable. Mike Love Collection

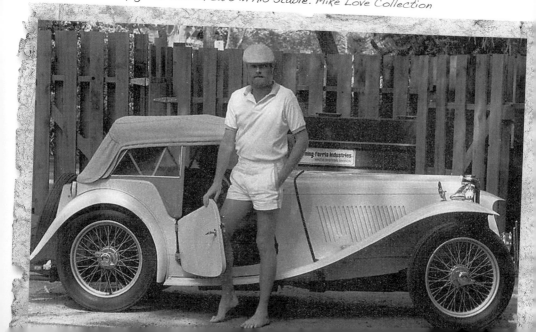

"It was definitely used, and it was the color green. And you know how people back in those days, they named their cars? Well, mine was 'Gangreen'—as in the disease. And every night on stage now, I say, 'I love my 1949 Chevy. Of course, not as much as I love my new Bentley!'

"I know I was in high school, so it might have been 1958. The Beach Boys didn't start until '61. I graduated in 1959. Nowadays on stage, we'll talk about our song called 'The Ballad of Ole' Betsy,' which is about a car that you really love, but it's getting a little raggedy, it's getting a little older. And some of the lyrics, 'She maybe rusted iron, but to me she's solid gold. I just can't hold the tears back because Betsy's growing old.'

"It's written by Roger Christian, who was co-writer with Brian on that song, and a DJ in Los Angeles during the '60s, and he wrote the words to 'Little Deuce Coupe,' 'The Ballad of Ole' Betsy,' and 'Don't Worry Baby' as well.

"I don't remember what they called my particular model. It was a '49 Chevy. It had a sloped back, and it was stick shift and six cylinders, and it was not exactly a dream car. It wasn't pretty, but it got the job done. Actually, I liked the body style. It's just that, rather than stay with it, as soon as we started the Beach Boys and started making some money, I bought a Jaguar sedan, which I drove all over the country—the Western part of the United States—to do shows. I took the seat out on the other side, not the driver's side obviously, and made it into a bed. I went with a friend of mine and we'd drive out to New Mexico, and up to Nevada, and all over the place to do these shows, because in those days we would travel a couple hundred miles between shows and do things at, like, an Indian reservation or a ballroom. Stuff like that. I didn't take my '49 Chevy. I sold that. I took my Jaguar 3.8 sedan.

"I worked at my dad's sheetmetal factory in East Los Angeles. He actually let me drive his 1958 pickup, and it was black with three dual carburetors. It hauled ass. Although it wasn't my first car, it was my first experience driving a really hot car. Three dual carburetors.

"I saved up some money and I bought my first car. My parents didn't buy me a car. They made me work for it, so I did. I eventually saved a few hundred dollars and bought that car used. I think it was like $600 or something that like. It wasn't a lot of money. There are stories about what went on in that car, but I'm not going to kiss and tell. It was during my senior year in high school.

"The steering column–mounted shifter broke, and I had to take the floorboard up and worked up a little contraption where I could shift on the floor, going direct to the gearbox. It was kind of funky. The mechanism that allowed you to shift from the steering wheel broke one piece at a time, and then for a while there I went through the floorboard and got to the gearbox and was able to shift it from there. It was pretty messed up.

"The car had the name 'Gangreen' on it. I painted the word 'Gangreen' on the left rear fender. The whole car needed paint, but I put 'Gangreen' on it because it was green and funky. And I put mud flaps on it too, which was kind of cool. Very East L.A.

"I lived in West Los Angeles, but in East L.A., they had a lot of lowrider type cars going around. I just emulated them by getting some mud flaps on mine.

"It wasn't fast; it was a little bit loud. It wasn't pretty, but it got the job done, and actually I like the style. In fact, over the years I've thought it would be nice to find a really cherry condition '49 Chevy and just have it to drive. It's very nostalgic. So I'll be on the lookout for something really good.

"We're playing a show in October called Cruisin' the Coast in Biloxi, Mississippi, that's similar to Hot August Nights in Reno, where they have all the classic cars come out. And so I'll be out looking for that '49 Chevy! It's not the most glamorous car ever. A lot of people don't restore them, but it was cool looking, I thought.

"I loved it because it was my first car, and I won't say hate, but it wasn't the fastest thing on wheels, that's for sure. So when you're a young guy and you like to think your car would beat anybody, but it wouldn't.

"For instance, a friend of mine had a '57 Chevy convertible. David Saul went to Dorsey High School with me, and THAT was a hot car. I didn't drive it. I drove in it with him. Oh, it was gorgeous. A '57 Chevy convertible. Red and chrome. It was beautiful. Classic.

"He was a very nice guy. His father owned a couple supermarkets in L.A., and so he was well taken care of. My dad had a sheetmetal factory, along with my grandfather and uncle, so we were more

"It wasn't fast; it was a little bit loud. It wasn't pretty, but it got the job done, and actually I like the style."

working class people. I grew up in Baldwin Hills and went to Dorsey High School in Los Angeles.

"It was nice just to be able to get around, go to games. My cousin, Beach Boy Brian (Wilson), had a Nash Rambler that was his first car.

"I graduated to a little Volkswagen Beetle and I remember I'd drive over to the Wilsons' house, and Brian and I wrote our first song called 'Surfin' in 1961, and it came out in the fall of '61. That was our first record release, in 1961. I was 20 years old.

"It was a big deal—having a car was the biggest deal for a young guy that possibly could be. I don't remember all that much more about that car.

"At one time, in 1965, I had a 1948 MG, a 1939 Rolls-Royce, a 1966 Jaguar XKE, and a yellow Jaguar four-door sedan. So I had the four British cars—the MG, the Rolls-Royce, the Jaguar sedan, and the Jaguar XKE, which was a beautiful car. Except for the Rolls-Royce, they were all yellow. That was the year—1965 was the year 'California Girls' came out.

"After three years of the Beach Boys touring and recording, we had enough money to buy to any car we wanted. My cousin Carl got an Aston Martin DB5. All the Beach Boys had Rolls-Royces, Corvettes. Carl had the Aston Martin, and I had the Jaguar XKE. That was pretty cool."

One wonders how Love and the rest of the band members traveled their band gear around in so many small British sports cars—not a Ford Woody wagon in sight. ∎

—As Told to K.S. Wang

NEIL PEART
1969 MGB

Many rock and roll drummers consider Peart the drummer they most want to be able to play like. Neil Peart, whose given first name is Cornelius, is one of the most universally respected rock drummers, and is best known for his nearly superhuman, pyrotechnic drum playing and for providing intellectual lyrics. Neil has served as both drummer and lyricist for the rock band Rush since 1975, with bassist/vocalist Geddy Lee and guitarist Alex Lifeson. (Rush's lineup has remained unchanged since Neil's arrival in 1975.) Rush is the most successful Canadian music group in history and is the third most prolific seller of consecutive (American) Gold and Platinum Records and videos, behind only the Beatles and the Rolling Stones. Beginning on August 10, 1997, immediately following Rush's Test For Echo tour, Neil Peart endured concurrent, seemingly unendurable tragedies when his daughter (and only child) died in a car accident, and his wife died from cancer 10 months later. This put Rush on indefinite hiatus for the first time and prompted Neil to write Ghost Rider: Travels on the Healing Road, *his second book. In September 2000, Neil married Los Angeles photographer Carrie Nuttall. Following Neil's recovery, Rush returned victoriously to the studio and the stage in 2002 with* Vapor Trails.

"My mother says my first word was 'car,' and I believe it. In an old photo album, there's a black-and-white, crinkle-cut snapshot of a one-year-old me sitting behind the wheel of Dad's '48 Pontiac. My chubby hands are gripping the rim of the wheel, and I am grinning at the camera.

In the middle of the dashboard of that car was a big, circular, chrome trim around the radio speaker, and when I rode on the bench seat between Mom and Dad, I 'steered' with that wheel.

Growing up in St. Catharines, Ontario, through the '50s and '60s, my treasures were Dinky Toys, Corgi Toys, and the gorgeous plastic promotional models—1/25 scale I think—that Dad would bring me and my brother, Danny, from the annual new car show across the border in Buffalo. I knew the model and year of every car on the road and had a collection of car badges and bits of chrome trim. Railroad crossings were good places to collect them. I considered it significant that in those locations I found more pieces that had fallen off of Chrysler products. I built models of hot rods and customs, and my bedroom walls were papered with center spreads from car magazines—lots of dragsters, from a magazine I believe was called *Car Craft*. There was also a big yellow poster with cutouts of Corvettes I made for a school project, on the history of 'America's sports car'—the centerpiece being the most recent model at the time, one that is still an all-time favorite, the '63 split-window. I could draw that car, and the '65 Mustang fastback, *perfectly* on the covers of my school notebooks.

"My friend Chad Smith from the Red Hot Chili Peppers has a beautiful black '63 'Vette, and one day, up at the Drum Channel studios in Oxnard, California, he parked it beside my '64 Aston Martin DB5, making a fetching portrait of mid-60s glamour.

"And speaking of drums and drummers, while it's true that cars pretty much dominated the first thirteen years of my life; well, along with birds and books; when I discovered the drums, everything— I mean *everything*—changed. Now instead of drawing Corvettes and Mustangs on the covers of my notebooks, I was drawing Keith Moon's drumset.

"Through my teenage years, in the late '60s and early '70s, I was a struggling musician. All my interest was focused on music, and all the money I could earn from lawn-mowing, working at my father's farm equipment dealership, and playing occasional gigs in church halls and high school gymnasiums, went to cymbals, drumheads, and sticks. I rode around in vans full of guitars, amplifiers, Hammond organs, and drums, but never thought of having a car of my own—never even got my license.

"My early twenties were spent in England, still a struggling musician, and cars remained on my radar—noticing the real British 'exotics,' like Marcos, Bristol, and TVR, seeing my first Lamborghini—the Espada, which I still covet as a formative dream car—and my first Aston Martin, the original DBS. It was owned by the boss at my day-job, selling souvenirs on Carnaby Street. He grumbled about that car, 'They should have stuck to making tractors.'

Peart and friend wheeling his MGB, top down, sun shining. Neal Peart

Only a true petrol-head—or a farm equipment dealer's son—would even get that reference.

"When I was 22, back in Canada and working at my dad's farm equipment dealership (and playing in local bands at night), he and I were driving through the local import dealer's lot in St. Catharines, Ontario, one Sunday. We just cruised through, having a look at the fancy foreign Jaguars, Triumphs, and MGs. Partly hidden alongside the sales building was a forlorn-looking little sports car—it sat a little wrong, like maybe one of the tires was flat or its suspension was wonky.

"It was a 1969 MGB roadster, British Racing Green, and I was *smitten*. My dad had a friend who worked for an affiliated dealership, and he gave me his best price: $1,900. Taking out a bank loan—*savings*? Ha!—I had just enough extra to display my budding hippie rock musician's flair and independent streak and had it painted metallic purple. Now that I had a car, it was time to finally get my driver's license—taking the driving test with Dad's big Ford wagon.

"Nowadays, it is strange for me to reflect that that MG was only four years old at the time—because it fully represented the cliché that 'old English sports cars' *still* exemplify. Temperamental, unreliable, prone to overheating and unexplained battery discharge, sweating oil from every pore, losing its composure in any wet or snowy conditions, and dying just when you need it most—in a word, maddening.

"Of course, MGs had the famous electrics by Lucas (the Prince of Darkness). My fellow local British car owners, with MGs, Triumphs, and Healeys, always wondered why cars made in *England* would die in the rain—or the car wash. The exhaust system dangled low, always catching on things, so you had to carry wire coat hangers in the 'boot' for emergency repairs—along with a full toolbox; spare spark plugs, points, and condenser; booster cables; and assorted specialized items. I still possess a small combination wrench, cut in half with a grinder, to fit one of the three thermostat housing bolts on an MGB engine.

"I learned *everything* from that car. The joys of driving, and the frustrations of the MG's primitive, agricultural technology. I replaced the entire exhaust system, performed regular oil changes, and with a more knowledgeable friend guiding me, even did a complete valve job on the engine, right down to the head gasket—which had been warped by an episode of terminal overheating.

"After a couple of years, I sold that MG to buy a Lotus Europa, soon learning to understand the Lotus owners' favorite acronym: Lots Of Trouble, Usually Serious. When my dad—who had progressed up the domestic-car ladder through full-size Buicks, Chevys, and Ford wagons—first saw the Lotus, he said, 'You really prefer that to a *real* car?'

"I said I did."

Peart still loves cars, but a busy world touring schedule doesn't allow him much time to enjoy them as a hobby. ∎

—As told to Tara Weingarten

Patrick Dempsey

1972 MERCEDES-BENZ 240D

Patrick Dempsey is likely best known for his role as Dr. "McDreamy" Derek Shepherd in the long-running television series Grey's Anatomy. *Dempsey's earliest film roles were in the mid-1980s, he made several appearances on the television series* Fast Times *in 1986, and he continues to balance dual careers in film and television. Dempsey is also a committed automotive enthusiast, a professional sports car racing driver, and racing team co-owner. His Dempsey Racing team currently competes in the Rolex Grand-Am series. Dempsey has raced in the Rolex 24 Hours of Daytona and the 24 Hours of Le Mans, driving his GT-Class Mazda RX-8. Dempsey owns several Mercedes-Benzs, a Jaguar XK-140, and a Ferrari Daytona, along with other collectible cars.*

TV dream idol or not, no dilettante racer is Patrick Dempsey.
His Grand-Am series GT-class team Mazda RX-8 placed third in
class in the Rolex 24 at Daytona endurance race in January 2011.
Al Merion, courtesy Mazda Motorsport

"It was brown. And it was slow. I bought it when I was 15. I lived in Maine, so it was a chore to drive a diesel in the cold weather because you had to heat up the glow plugs to start it. I've always been fascinated with Mercedes-Benz, and I have several now. I think I paid $2,500 for it, which was a lot of money for a kid. It was everything I had saved up. It was fun because it was a great date car; you showed up in a Mercedes and the girls were impressed. I loved that car, but it always broke down at the most inopportune time. One time, it broke down and because I was with something that I had a relationship with, it changed my life, in some ways that were very positive and in others that were very negative.

"I kept it until I was 19. I remember I was on tour with a production of *Brighton Beach Memoirs*, and then I was doing a movie in Montreal, and then I drove it back to New York. I remember I was in West Point and it just died on me. I sold it to a local, probably for next to nothing. In hindsight, I learned a lot from that relationship. I think about that car in context because Mercedes is now such a world leader in diesel technology.

"After that, I bought my '63 Porsche 356B convertible with all the money I made from one movie. The Porsche was used as the "sound car" for the making of *Top Gun*. Remember the Porsche that the Kelly McGillis character drove? The engine sounds on the film's soundtrack were made by my car. It was the only car I had, and it was my daily driver for 10 years. And I still have it, and I'll never sell it." ∎

BRANFORD MARSALIS
Nissan 280 ZX

Branford Marsalis is a saxophonist, composer, and former leader of NBC's The Tonight Show *Band. Branford Marsalis is the eldest son in the "first family of jazz." Born August 26, 1960, Marsalis is a musical iconoclast and occasional actor. He has collaborated with many greats, such as Herbie Hancock, Art Blakey, Terence Blanchard, Sting, Guru, Miles Davis, Bruce Hornsby, brother Wynton, and other members of his family. He was the original bandleader for* The Tonight Show *with Jay Leno for nearly three years until he walked away to return to his love, jazz music.*

> ## "So then I turn on the windshield wipers and they don't work. That's when I start to notice that there's no molding on the window on the passenger side, so water is leaking into the car and all over me."

"Ed, my former manager, had a 280 ZX Nissan. He was just starting to do well, so he bought a Peugot 505, and he was moving his operations from Boston to D.C. I was talking about learning how to drive a stick shift. He says, 'I have an old Nissan. Why don't you take it back to New York with you?' Great. So I spent two days in Boston, riding around, learning how to drive a stick. Finally I leave. I'm about 40 minutes into the ride and suddenly a huge, torrential downpour hits. It's that kind of rain you can't see five feet in front of you. So then I turn on the windshield wipers and they don't work. That's when I start to notice that there's no molding on the window on the passenger side, so water is leaking into the car and all over me. The windows start to fog up. I turn something on, and hot air blows through, and it was like a blanket of mosquitoes covered the window. So I'm on this road, going 40 miles an hour, all this water, the windshield wipers don't work, and I'm driving this car in third gear. And a routine, four-hour trip took seven hours!

Marsalis may have left his manager's "not so classic" 280 ZX abandoned on the highway, but he is never far away from his tenor saxophone. Marsalis paid to replace the car and then replaced the manager. Copyright Samuel Goldwyn Films/Everett Collection

"Right in the middle of that one lane, it conked out."

"I finally get to New York, and I park the car in front of my house. I get up the next day, it won't start. I mean, the third day I've got the damn thing, it won't start. So I bring it to the shop, and they say it's the starter. Two hundred and thirty-five dollars. Bang! Gone! Drive the sucker around for another month. It keeps stopping. Take it to the shop, they don't know what it is. It could be the alternator. It still stops. Then they say it may be the battery. They replace the battery and still it stops. And I'm calling Ed the whole while saying, 'Hey, this car is messing up!' And he says, 'Well, it never messed up on me, man. You must be doing something wrong.' This went on for five months. I had to replace all the parts. Everything!

"One day, I was on the Brooklyn Queens Expressway, on the way to watch the Mets play, and there is a point at which it merges and goes from three lanes to one lane and then back again to three. Right in the middle of that one lane, it conked out. I got out of the car and I pushed it over to the neutral zone, jumped off the bridge, called a taxi, went to Shea Stadium, and just left that car sitting there. Never to be seen again.

"About eight months later, Ed calls me and says, 'Where's my car, man?'

"'You're joking. Right?' I say to him. 'It's somewhere on the BQE!'"

"He tells me, 'It's a classic car!'

"And I say, 'Yeah. Right. Sure. It would have been with maybe $8,000 of work.'

"He says: 'Since you lost my car, I think I should be duly compensated.'

"I paid him, like, $100,000 for the car just so he would leave me alone. Then I got a new manager." ∎

BUD BRUTSMAN
1969 Ford Mustang Mach 1

Bud Brutsman is a television producer and series creator, living in Southern California. He has been the vision behind many automotive-related documentary shows, and is an avid off-road/Baja racer.

"I grew up as a very ambitious, rambunctious teenager in the early '80s in Cheyenne, Wyoming. I was a bit high strung; what you'd call a troubled youth. I was arrested for stealing an L88 Corvette, and was an all-around crazy kid.

"My father and I didn't have the best relationship. You know how it is when you're 15—you know everything and your dad knows nothing. I grew up in what I now know was a pretty cool household. Dad was an engineer and built stock cars, and my brother was a hot rodder. He always drove Mustangs. So I was surrounded by motor-heads, but I was way too radical to care, and went around doing my own thing.

"Like many fathers, he isn't a great communicator and had to work hard just to muster up an 'I love you' every quarter or so. On Christmas Day 1985, I remember being in the den of our house. I was 15 at the time, about five months prior to turning 16, and being able to get my driver's license. My dad told me he had one more gift for me, and points out to the barn. We lived in a rural area on about five acres, and had a real barn on our property. I looked outside, and could see the tail panel of a '69 Mustang Mach 1. I couldn't believe it and went running outside even though the snow was several feet deep.

"It was Acapulco Blue with mustard yellow stripes and a white interior. My excitement faded quickly, because when I got to the passenger side of the car, it looked like it had been hit by a train. The entire side was caved in, like Garfield with his face pressed up against a window. My dad had been watching the whole scene from inside. My first comment after seeing the car is unprintable, and then I looked at him like 'What the %*#@ is this!?' He was happy for a moment, but once my expression registered with him, I could see from his body language that he know this arrogant, pompous, 15-year-old just didn't get it. I absolutely didn't have a clue about what he was hoping to accomplish.

"I went back inside and said, 'Dad, you know the Mustang is a unibody car, and we're never going to be able to fix it from a hit like that and make it right. There's nobody on the planet that makes reproduction parts for this car. Besides, I have things I need to do. I have to drink and I have girls I have to chase. I need reliable transportation.' My dad tried to convince me that it would be a great summer project, and we can fix it—together. The last thing you want to do when you're 15 is spend your whole summer in the garage with your dad and a body hammer. I couldn't think of anything worse.

"About three months later, I was thrown out of high school, became an emancipated minor, and left home. My parents thought I'd go out there, see how tough life was, then move back in and live happily under their rules. But I never went back, being pretty bent on being to make it on my own. I moved to California, and ultimately began working in television.

"I created a show called *Rides*, then another called *Overhaulin'*—the latter being inspired by something I call the Friday night thrash. When I was a kid, everybody in town used to race on Saturday nights at a small track in Cheyenne called Big Country Speedway. Everyone worked full-time jobs, and there wasn't a lot of money around. The cars were the usual—Camaros, Chevelles, and such. No matter what happened with them and which one got wrecked, all the guys who could fabricate or weld would cruise to whoever's house on Friday night and get the cars ready for Saturday. We'd work all night to get the cars back on track. It all happened in the course of a week, which if you are familiar with *Overhaulin'*, you'll recognize a similar formula.

"*Hot Rod* magazine did an article about me and our several shows, nicknaming me the King of Car TV. Then I was out on the *Hot Rod* Power Tour, and actor/TV host Christopher Titus came up and called me a poseur. 'How can you be the King of Car TV in *Hot Rod* if you don't even own a hot rod?' He was right.

"I called Kevin King, president of Year One [a maker of muscle car restoration parts and accessories] and probably my best friend, and said, 'I want to build a hot rod. Let's build a car together.' Kevin, being

Not the Christmas present a young Bud Brutsman was expecting.
Bud Brutsman collection

The Mach I had taken a hard hit, but fortunately wasn't beyond saving.
Its restoration, in partnership with Brutsman's father, is nearly
complete. Bud Brutsman collection

Brutsman with another, and very different, Mustang Mach I, a car he calls "Blackened" which was built in concert with friends Chip Foose and Kevin King. Randy Lorentzen

the Can-Do guy of all Can-Do guys, said 'Great. What do you want to build?' Something inside me told me I just had to build a '69 Mustang, in homage to my first '69 that my dad gave me in 1985, although we never fixed it up. After looking at all kinds of cars, we came around to two important criteria: it had to be a '69 Mach 1 fastback, and it had to be black.

"We got sponsors together. Chip Foose helped out and put some touches on it and built me some special wheels for it. When we were done, I had—for me, anyway—the coolest '69 Mustang on the planet. Black chrome, supercharged 4.6-liter Ford motor, roll cage, you name it; it's an unbelievable car. *Hot Rod* magazine did a feature on it. I've got a great car, it's in *Hot Rod*, my life is fulfilled, right? Not quite.

"As fabulous as it is, what I began to realize is that this car was a failed attempt to fill a hole in my heart. Producing more and more episodes of *Overhaulin'*, which isn't really a car show, but a 'people stories' show, also made me realize why I was unsatisfied. The black car filled my need to have a hot rod, but there was something else that this car, and no other car, could accomplish. Then it hit me.

"In 1985, my dad wasn't trying to give me reliable transportation. With that whole deal, he was trying to reach out to this troubled, stubborn, arrogant 15-year-old kid. He wanted to put his time and effort and muscle into fixing this Mustang up with me so that when his kid went to high school, he'd look like a stud. He was reaching out to me. And I missed it. It's frustrating to me, and I wish I would have done it differently and maybe things would have been better. You can't second-guess yourself, and you can't turn back the clock. But there was something I could do.

"Fortunately, Dad still had the Mach 1. Twenty-three years had gone by, and it was still sitting in exactly the same place, out beside our barn. In July 2008, we threw chains around it, pulled it out of the yard, and sent it to Gateway Classic Mustang in Missouri, run by the Childress family. I told my dad that we were going to rebuild that car. Fortunately, the parts situation is much better than it was back then. Gateway is doing the work, but my dad and I are picking colors, we're talking about motors and suspension, what kind of dash we're going to have in it. He's kind of old school, and some of the stuff he wants to do with it is a little dated, but it doesn't matter. We'll both own it, we'll both drive it; we'll share it.

"So I still have my first car, and after nearly 25 years, I'm getting to fulfill that car's original prophecy, the one that I screwed up so bad the first time around. Fortunately I had the opportunity to right the situation. And my father and I will be closer together because of it."

A much humbler Brutsman, now married and a father of his own son, continues to develop innovative automotive television. ■

"After looking at all kinds of cars, we came around to two important criteria: it had to be a '69 Mach 1 fastback, and it had to be black."

Running on
All Cylinders

ATHLETES

Bill Goldberg

1976 PONTIAC TRANS-AM

Goldberg, as he was called in the ring, is a two-time WWE champion and also won a WCW championship. Since retiring from the NFL and from professional wrestling, a committed car guy, Bill Goldberg has forged a career as an actor and television personality, hosting several different programs for SPEED TV.

> *"When I was 16, my dad said, 'Get a 3.0 GPA and a job, and I'll get you a car.' I had a 2.9 and I got a job at McDonalds, so he got me a car."*

"It was in a lot better shape when I got it than when I got rid of it. It was a 1976 Pontiac Trans-Am. It wasn't exactly what I wanted, but it was a nice first car, for sure. I think that started my 'addiction' to cars. My family has an affinity for automobiles. When I was 16, my dad said, 'Get a 3.0 GPA and a job, and I'll get you a car.' I had a 2.9 and I got a job at McDonalds, so he got me a car. And I've had a lot of cars come and go since then, including a Boss 429 Mustang, a '70 Camaro Z28, a '68 Camaro, and several Mopars." ■

Bill Goldberg is a big guy, and goes for big cars, especially those with big engines and big horsepower. Catherine Harrell

Dan Jansen

CHEVROLET MALIBU

A many-times record holder in speed skating, Jansen competed four times in the Olympic Games, finally winning the gold in the 1,000-meter event in 1994 and setting a world record. Jansen was inducted into the United States Olympic Hall of Fame in 2004. Today, Jansen is a speed skating commentator for NBC and, from 2005–2007, the skating coach for the Chicago Blackhawks of the National Hockey League.

Today, Jansen relies more on his BMW's all-wheel drive than the two slender blades of steel that carried him to so many speed skating wins. Catherine Harrell

Excerpted with permission from How Athletes Roll by Barbara Terry, copyright 2010 by Barbara Terry.

"I shared a car with my brother, because I'm the youngest of nine kids, and we didn't have a lot of money. The first one my dad bought us, because we were training and we needed to get to our workouts, I think it was a Chevy Malibu. It was this green thing with a white top and he paid $300 for it. We'd get so frustrated because we'd pull up to a stoplight, and as soon as you hit the gas, for whatever reason, it would stall. We would get stuck in intersection after intersection as the light turned green and it would stall. But that was pretty much our first car, you know, *mine*, where I had to pay for gas and do what I did to get where I had to go. Other than hand-me-downs, what was the first car that I bought for myself? First car that I purchased? It was a Chrysler LeBaron. No reason; I started saving money to buy a car. And it wasn't the old boxy kind, like when Chrysler started making their comeback. It was a sportier car, but it was nothing special. But it was nice." ∎

"We'd get so frustrated because we'd pull up to a stoplight, and as soon as you hit the gas, for whatever reason, it would stall."

RAY "BOOM BOOM" MANCINI
1970s Pontiac LeMans

Ray "Boom Boom" Mancini is a retired American boxer and former World Boxing Association lightweight champion, a title he held for two years in the 1980s. Born in Youngstown, Ohio, boxing was a big part of the Mancini family history. Mancini's father, Lenny Mancini (the original "Boom Boom"), was a top-ranked contender during the 1940s who was widely predicted to be a future world champion. His hopes were crushed after being wounded in World War II. Although he returned to boxing, his injuries and physical limits kept him from reaching his potential. His son, Ray, had a stellar career on the amateur circuit, and in 1978, he made the jump to the professional ranks and became WBA lightweight champion in 1982. Mancini officially retired in 1992, leaving a record of 29–5, with 23 knockouts. Ray Mancini is also the nephew of award-winning composer Henry Mancini.

A young Mancini at the dawn of his legendary career. Ray Mancini

"I was a sophomore in high school. And in those days, in Youngstown, Ohio, you needed a car to get around. My parents couldn't pay for my insurance, and my parents couldn't pay for the gas. I had to do that, and so I had get a job.

"I was a busboy at Fonderlac Country Club. My mother had a friend at a church hall that served dinners, and if there were banquets she would be the caterer for that hall. So I was busboy and dishwasher for her. It wasn't every weekend. For her, it was a couple times a month, and as a busboy I worked three times a week. So I saved enough money to pay for the car. I had a friend who was selling a Pontiac LeMans for $100. I don't remember why he was selling it, but $100 sounded like a deal to me. It was a good looking car.

"It was yellow with a black top. I called it the 'Yellowjacket.' It was used but a new car for me. I started to date at the time, and you can't have your mom and dad take you out on dates. My first couple of dates, they did. My parents would take me some place. Her parents would take her some place. It's not too romantic. At that time, when you're 16, you start driving, you want to get a job, you want to have extra money—you've got to have a car to get to your job. Your parents can't drop you off and pick you up for long—you can only do that once in a while.

"It overheated in the middle of the freeway at night after a couple months. The radiator was shot. A friend of mine said it was cracked, it leaked water. I was walking on the freeway at night, trying to find a call box to call my mom to come pick me up. But a stranger drove by and I told him that I was looking for a call box, so he drove me. I called my mother and they came and got me. We left the car on Highway 680 in Youngstown overnight then picked it up the next morning.

"I loved it because it was mine. When it's your first car, you're attached to it. Of course I loved that car. And then with the radiator overheating, and then steaming, I didn't hate anything else about it, other than it had a cracked radiator. And it broke down on the highway. It got like an old bird; she just didn't have it no more. When an old car is just limping around, you have to put it out of its misery eventually.

"That was the spring of '77 when I had that car. I bought it and my birthday was in March. After I broke down on the highway, I always kept a jug full of water and if it started to steam, I pulled over, put the water in, let it sit for five minutes, and then drove. I think I took it to the scrap-metal house and they paid me whatever they could give me for scrap metal. That's how I got rid of it. That was about four or five months after I broke down on the highway. I was driving like a victim, keeping water in the car. Because if you're waiting for something to happen, you're just driving like a victim.

"I had that car for almost a year and then I bought a used Chevy for $60 during my junior year in high school. So the total of my first two cars was a buck 60! The Chevy lasted me a couple years. I have all my cars nicknamed. When I got the blue Chevy Impala, I called it the 'Blue Streak.'

"The Blue Streak was the best car I ever had. That car lasted me for 14 months, for 60 bucks. It had no heater; it had no air conditioner. During winter, I had to stick my head out of the window to see when the windows were too fogged up. If the window got too frozen, I tried to scrape it, and if I couldn't scrape it, then I had to stick my head out the window to drive.

"I used to go through the snowdrifts in it. The tires I got were so bald, I used to slip and slide, fishtailing all over the place. You gotta understand, those days, how lucky I was. We didn't wear seatbelts then. I'm so happy it's mandatory now for my children that are driving. I couldn't even foresee that we'd be driving with our seatbelts on. I was so lucky, we all were lucky, since none of the kids in my generation wore seatbelts."

Mancini's career was cut short after he fought Korean boxer Duk Koo Kim in 1982. Kim passed away shortly thereafter, and Mancini was unfairly blamed for the incident. Mancini attempted a brave comeback, but it wasn't the same, and he remained burdened by Kim's passing, and retired for the final time in 1992. ■

—AS TOLD TO K.S. WANG

Arnold Palmer

1949 FORD SEDAN

Arnold Palmer is among the world's best known athletes, and one of the most popular golfers of all-time. He's notched victories in seven of golf's "major" tourneys, including four Masters, winning the U.S. Open in 1960, and two wins in the British Open. Since retirement from golf, Palmer has become a successful businessman, owned numerous automobile dealerships, has designed golf courses, and is also an avid aviator.

My first car was a 1949 Ford two-door Ford Sedan. I bought it with my own money, as I have with every car or every mode of transportation that I have ever had. Today, I drive mostly Cadillacs, and my favorite mode of transportation is my Citation 10 jet. ■

Today, Palmer pedals golf carts and old tractors on the golf course, plus his Citation jet. Catherine Harrell

Excerpted with permission from How Athletes Roll by Barbara Terry, copyright 2010 by Barbara Terry.

Mike Piazza

1972 CHEVY NOVA

A Pennsylvania native, Mike Piazza is an All-Star catcher and power hitter. Piazza was drafted in the 62nd round of the 1988 amateur draft (the 1,390th player overall); he beat the odds and made it to the major leagues, becoming the National League rookie of the year for the Los Angeles Dodgers in 1993. In 1999 he signed a then groundbreaking seven-year, $91 million contract with the New York Mets; the next year he helped the Mets into the World Series, where they were defeated by Derek Jeter and the New York Yankees. Piazza's rugged good looks have made him one of the Internet's favorite sports heartthrobs. Piazza has played 16 seasons of Major League Baseball, is a 12-time all-star, and is a surefire Hall of Famer. He is one of the best-hitting catchers of all time.

Not a Chevy Nova to be seen in this photo of the now retired baseball great, with his Mercedes-Benz S-Class and Range Rover. Catherine Harrell

Excerpted with permission from How Athletes Roll by Barbara Terry, copyright 2010 by Barbara Terry.

> *"I mean, my first job, when I was 12 years old, was washing cars down at my dad's car lot, so I was driving around the parking lot when I was 14."*

"It was a '72 Nova. It was kind of neat. It had the air shocks in the back that you adjusted with an air hose. It was red. My father was in the car business, so we always had a plethora of cars around, and the Nova was a trade-in. I only had it for a couple of months, and then I just started looking around at other cars. I would be at my dad's dealership when a trade-in would come in, and then I would drive the salesmen crazy because they wanted to resell all of the trade-ins, but I wanted dibs on some of them. Then I had an IROC Z Camaro, which was also a trade-in. The Sport model with a T-top and stuff. That was standard issue in high school for me. What else did we have? We had a bunch of stuff. The good thing about being in the car business was that you get so many trade-ins. I mean, my first job, when I was 12 years old, was washing cars down at my dad's car lot, so I was driving around the parking lot when I was 14. I've always loved cars, and it is such a big part of my family history. I also have an affinity for those late '60s muscle cars—Camaros, GTOs, Chevelles. ∎

BRUCE JENNER
1954 Cadillac Hearse

*Bruce Jenner twice represented the United States at the Olympics—
1972 and 1976—when he won the gold medal in the grueling 10-phase
decathlon, and was named Athlete of the Year by the Associated Press.
After he retired from Olympic competition, Jenner dabbled in professional sports car racing, and has become an actor and popular reality
television personality.*

Jenner's Hearse and IMSA GTO-class Mustang racer have given
way to more sedan street rides, such as his current S-Class.
Catherine Harrell

"I thought my first car was going to be an Austin-Healey Sprite, but I have a tragic story relating to that car. My dad taught me how to drive in Tarrytown, New York, in a grocery store parking lot.

"I was 15 turning 16. And he had a little Austin-Healey "bugeye" Sprite. It was red with white stripes. And it was the coolest little car; a convertible. It was a four-speed, so he taught me how to drive a stick shift down in the parking lot. That was probably three or four months before I got my license. Of course, I snuck it out a few times when he wasn't around. We lived in an apartment complex and I drove it around the apartment complex and never got caught. My sister got caught because she bumped into a car, but that's another story. The day I got my license, my dad sold the car.

"Yes, when I got home from getting my license, all excited, my dad said, 'I sold the car today.' I was devastated. About a month ago I was driving past a used car lot and saw a bugeye Austin-Healey Sprite. I wanted to go in and buy the thing and paint it red, and fix it up, detail it out, just so I would have it. So that was a pretty tragic start to the car world for me."

The Sprite was a very compact, short-wheelbased roadster; one wonders how comfortable the lanky, 6'2" Jenner would have been in this car on long trips? It's doubtful he would have event fit inside with the convertible top in the closed position.

"If I was good, my dad would let me drive a Ford Falcon station wagon. And he would let me drive the car when I was good—only when I was good—so I never had a car when I was young. But then, when I was 18, I guess, this friend of ours had a 1954 Cadillac hearse in the backyard and he wanted to get rid of it, so he says, 'I'll give it to you for $150.' I snatched that baby right up. So when I had about six months left in my senior year in high school, I got my first car and it was a '54 Cadillac hearse. One time I think we had 24 people back in the hearse—my record—coming home from a party."

Jenner knows cars and knows how to drive. He raced professionally for Roush Racing on the IMSA motorsport circuit in the mid-1980s, posting a GTO class win at Sebring in 1986. He's known today to younger audiences as the Kardashian sisters' step-father on the reality television series, *Keeping Up with the Kardashians.* ■

Natalie Gulbis

1983 FORD BRONCO

Natalie Gulbis played her first LPGA event at the age of 14 (making her, at the time, the youngest player to qualify for an LPGA tourney), previously playing high school golf on the boys team, turning pro at 18 while in college. She loves all manner of cars, trucks, and muscle cars, and works on motorcycles with her father. Her first "non-truck" car is her current Lexus IS350 convertible. She also hosted her own golf-based reality television show in 1994, and appeared in the second season of reality show Celebrity Apprentice.

Gulbis is an attractive, capable, and popular player on the LPGA, and still owns her first car. Catherine Harrell

186

As told to Barbara Terry, excerpted from her book, How Athletes Roll

"*I prefer black cars, but also have a bright Ferrari-Red '68 Mustang fastback, which I keep at my parents' house in Sacramento, California.*"

"My first car was an '83 Ford Bronco. [I got it when] I was in college, my second semester. My parents bought me the Bronco; navy blue exterior with a tan interior. It was an Eddie Bauer and I loved it. I've always liked big trucks and cars. Then, when I turned professional, I bought a Tahoe. A 1999 two-door Chevy Tahoe, after which came a black Ford Harley-Davidson edition F-Series pickup. I prefer black cars, but also have a bright Ferrari-Red '68 Mustang fastback, which I keep at my parents' house in Sacramento, California." ∎

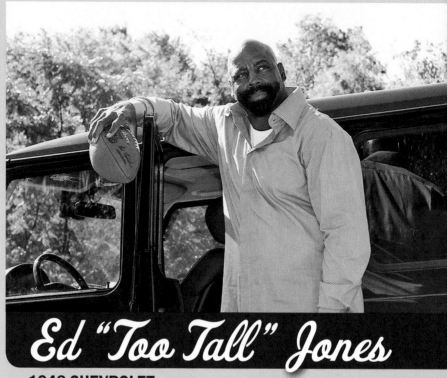

Ed "Too Tall" Jones

1948 CHEVROLET

Jones played 15 seasons—all with the Dallas Cowboys—in the NFL, taking one year off to try his hands at professional boxing. The 6'9", 270-plus-pound Jones was one of the most feared defensive linemen in the game, and earned three trips to the Pro Bowl, and played on the 1978 Super Bowl–winning team. Jones was given his nickname by critics who said that he was "too tall" to play football. His reputation as an effective lineman and enviable career record indicates otherwise.

Some said the near seven-foot-tall Jones was "too tall" to play football, hence his nickname. His impressive NFL, Super Bowl, and Pro Bowl record indicates otherwise. Catherine Harrell

"I would give anything to know where it is now, and I would try and buy it back."

"My first car was a 1948 Chevy. I used to watch the old gangster movies, like Eliot Ness, and I saw that car and absolutely loved it. There was a guy in Tennessee who was an antique collector, and I talked him into letting me buy his all-black 1948 Chevy. I would give anything to know where it is now, and I would try and buy it back. I had it all during college, and sold it when I finished school. When I graduated, I bought a new Cadillac Eldorado that I thought was just the most beautiful thing. Then I sold the 1948 Chevy." ■

John McEnroe

FORD PINTO

Winner of about every tennis award including three-time Wimbledon champ and four-time U.S. Men's Singles champ, John McEnroe is considered to be one of the greatest players of the game.

Excerpted with permission from How Athletes Roll by Barbara Terry, copyright 2010 by Barbara Terry.

> ## "I drove it around almost three years, and then sold it for about $50 to some people my parents knew."

"The first car I had was an old wreck, a Ford Pinto. My father bought it from one of the partners in his law firm. He paid $100 for it. It was four or five years old at that point and very beat up. I was 17. My parents had it painted orange before they gave it to me. I drove it around almost three years, and then sold it for about $50 to some people my parents knew. Their son drove it another few years.

"My next car, which I bought myself, was a Mercedes 450 SL." ∎

Opposite: McEnroe celebrates another Ace. His "Old wreck Pinto" didn't last too long; as soon as he had the money, the outspoken tennis great upgraded to a 450 SL. Craig Golding/Getty Images

5

The Rest of the Pack

JOURNALISTS, ARTISTS, AND OTHERS

DAVID E. DAVIS JR.
1935 Mercedes-Benz Roadster

Known to millions simply as "David E.," Mr. Davis is one of the deans of postwar automotive magazine journalism. He is unique among American motoring writers, having at one time or another worked at all of the Big Four monthlies: Car and Driver, *which he led through what many consider its finest years;* Road & Track, *where he began his career selling automotive advertising in the 1950s;* Motor Trend, *as editorial director; and* Automobile, *which he founded in 1986. He calls automotive icons like Bob Lutz, Carroll Shelby, and the late Juan Manuel Fangio his friends, and has written crisp, witty, well-thought prose about nearly every aspect of the motoring world for more than five decades.*

No, this isn't Mr. Davis' Mercedes-Benz or his MG, but a rather fine Ferrari Barchetta that he sampled for an article in Automobile magazine. Martyn Goddard

"My first car was a 1935 Mercedes-Benz roadster, purchased for $1,000 in 1951. An American colonel had brought it home from Germany, only to be defeated by its service needs. That car was my friend and constant companion for more than a year until I decided to become a racing driver and sold it to raise money for a competitive entry-level sports car. I was living in a very small town, a hundred miles from my parents and my childhood. I worked at a variety of jobs during the days, and drove to see friends, and farmland, and forests—and life—in the nights. The car ran like a train. It had a six-cylinder engine and an overdrive transmission. We were a team, that car and I. I accelerated through its gears, pushed the lever to the overdrive fourth gear, waited for a moment for it to engage, then droned across high-crowned, two-lane country roads in the gathering dark.

"The top was stowed behind the seats. The warm wind wrapped the back of my neck like a scarf, and the moon lit the backs of my hands on the steering wheel. The instruments glowed softly; barely legible in their faint yellow light. Sometimes I drove for miles without lights, just following the road by its contour and by the march of the utility poles stretching toward the ends of the earth in the moonlight.

"Going where? Going to see women who were sleepy and tousled and warm when I parked beneath their windows and walked quietly across the grass to their doors. Going to see old friends who wanted to drink and talk about women whom they used to visit in the night. Going to a gypsy restaurant where the owner played the violin, and his wife accompanied him on the accordion, and the hat-check girl loved me. Going to the right because that road led to a secluded lake. Going to the left because that road seemed to promise more curves. Going to the end of the road because I'd never been there before. Going to . . . I don't know where. Perhaps going to the future; to the rest of my life.

"Then there was the MG. White with black-edged yellow stripes over the louvered hood and front fenders. The grille painted checkerboard. The engine was tuned to its limit. The exhaust pipe was a copper tube, 1 1/2 inches in diameter. The sound was much greater than the performance, but to drive it fast was pure unbridled joy. The headlights were the best Marchals available at the time. On the badge bar stood a pair of Lucas flamethrowers that made the scenery of the night an all-flat white foreground, two dimensional, pierced by the reflected light of deer eyes in the forest that lined the road. My windscreen was folded down, and bugs stung my cheeks and forehead as I tore across the agricultural heartland.

"We drive cars because they make us free. With cars, we need not wait in airline terminals or travel only where the railway tracks go. Governments detest our cars; they give us too much freedom. How do you control people who can climb into a car at any hour of the day or night and drive to who knows where? An open car gives us another dimension of freedom. In an open car we enjoy the heightened freedom of the coursing hound, racing across the land with only the wind for clothing. It is the freedom of wild ducks, shining in their colorful plumage, flying at impossible speeds through the treetops to impress the duck-women they love. In a closed car, the world is a horizontal space, seen through windows that are too much like television screens. In an open car, the world becomes properly round above us, a vast dome of pure possibility, limited only by what we know of the universe. In an open car on an open road, we can feel what that man felt eons ago, when he first managed to grab a horse's mane, throw himself on its back, and feel himself transported at unthinkable speed into mankind's next stage of development." ∎

"Governments detest our cars; they give us too much freedom. How do you control people who can climb into a car at any hour of the day or night and drive to who knows where?"

JEFFREY R. ZWART
1970 Porsche 914-6

Jeff Zwart is one of the world's premiere automotive photographers and cinematographers. Most enthusiasts likely first saw his work in the pages of Road & Track *magazine. Zwart became enamored of hillclimb-style rally racing, then parked his cameras for occasional stints behind the wheel. His production company, Radical Media, has produced numerous documentaries and several television commercials and videos for clients such as Porsche and BMW.*

"Somewhere in the middle of Nicaragua, I was chasing former F1 and sports car racer Clay Regazzoni in his Mercedes 300 SEL rally car. It was day 3 of 25 of the Panama Alaska Rally. I was in my Porsche 914-6 and up ahead, Clay's Mercedes appeared to be wider than the broken little road we were racing on. Each time I got close to him, we could hear the roar of his big V-8 over the little six directly behind our heads. His car was slipping and sliding everywhere, and we were no match on the long straightaways to his V-8. My co-driver Martin Headland advised me that there was a town coming up and that could be our chance to get around Clay. Sure enough, the road tightened as we entered the town and we were able to close up on Clay as he careened across a narrow bridge. At another bridge, as we exited the town, we late braked into the bridge, and were now inches away from him as we watched him drift clear to the outside of the road as we exited off the bridge. Clay was trying to get his massive horsepower to the road and we dove inside him and never gave up staying on the pavement. My 914-6 was serving us well, only 22 more days to Alaska.

"It's hard to imagine that this 1970 Porsche 914-6 was my first car. The rally described above was in 1997, and I bought the car in 1974, so I had already had the car for 23 years before I converted it to a full FIA Rally Car. I had been running in the U.S. Pro Rally Championship with a Carrera 4, so when I heard about this long distance event it sparked my interest.

"As I grew up, I had a paper route and my dad required that I invest half my paper route money in the stock market each month.

Zwart then (top) and Zwart now (bottom). The man has grown up a bit and wears a bit less hair, but the car is the same. Jeff Zwart collection

Being a kid that loved sports, I invested in AMF—they made all the sports equipment that I seemed to be interested in. The deal was that I had to invest my money and leave it alone until after high school. All through high school I followed the exploits of Porsche and went to every race possible. I fell in love with the six-cylinder engine and that 'dry peas in a can' sound that came with it. [Porsche] 911s were every-where, but occasionally I would get to see a 914-6. The mid-engine configuration mated with the same six from the 911 seemed perfect to me. Another advantage was that they were not as popular as the 911 so they were cheaper.

"When I was finally out of high school, I could sell my stocks and spend the money—all I wanted was a 914-6. I found an ad in the *L.A. Times* for a low-mileage 914-6 offered for sale for $4,300. The guy who owed my car was a Ford dealer and he was taking delivery on a new Pantera. I remember going to his house and seeing the car; it was yellow and perfect. And the moment I started it, I knew it had to be mine. That six-cylinder was intoxicating and the fact it sat only about six inches behind my head made it all that more seductive.

"So here I was, an 18-year-old kid with a yellow 1970 Porsche 914-6. I also was interested in photography at the time, so I made it the subject of many photos as I went off to college in it and ultimately studied photography at Art Center in Pasadena. I started covering rallies for *Sports Car* magazine, which took myself and my 914-6 to some pretty obscure places. On one of my assignments, my throttle cable broke. It took quite a while to figure it out, but finally I was able to fix it by removing the speaker wire from one side of my speakers and splicing it into the throttle cable. It wasn't a perfect fix, but it got me home.

"Those days photographing rallies developed into a love of the sport, and meeting people like Rod Millen allowed me to even get closer to it. Rod built my first rally car, and in 1990 I was the Open Class National Champion in the SCCA Pro Rally Championship, tying for the overall championship. I went on to run with a Porsche Carrera 4 through 1994, at which time I started concentrating on the Pike's Peak International Hillclimb, all racing Porsches.

"In 1997 I heard about an FIA Marathon Rally that ran for 25 days covering 10,000 miles. It was a stage format rally so I knew it would be flat-out racing. The rules permitted 1972 and earlier cars so I decided to convert my very first car, my 914-6, into a full FIA spec rally car. I hated to potentially ruin this car that was so original and meant so much to me, but I knew if the car made it, it would only more endearing to me and have a little history at the same time. Well, 25 days later we rolled into Anchorage, and after battling 75 teams from all over the world, we had finished second overall, only being beat by a 911 from Australia.

"Thirty-five years later, I still have the car. It still makes that marvelous 'dry peas in a can' sound—albeit a little louder in rally spec. It was fully restored after the Panama Alaska Rally. My high school and college friends still ask if I have that yellow Porsche. It's still around and has a great story to tell."

Zwart continues to race Porsches, having enjoyed considerable success at Pike's Peak and other rally/hillclimb venues. ∎

John Glenn

1929 ROADSTER

John Glenn was the first man to orbit the planet Earth and became a U.S. Senator from Ohio, returning to space in his 70s as a space shuttle astronaut.

Young commander Glenn and guest appear to be swarmed by the early '60s version of the paparazzi. AP Photo/Ed Kolenovsky

"My dad gave me a dilapidated 1929 roadster when I was 16. It was a battered old car that I had painted bright red, and it had a canvas top that I always kept lowered. I named the car 'The Cruiser.' I was known as Bud at the time.

"My hometown is New Concord, Ohio, and it was a great place to grow up. I remember my friends would pile into The Cruiser for rides into the countryside or to the ice cream parlor, the Ohio Valley Dairy, on Main Street. My wife, Annie, and I had started going steady in the eighth grade, and always ordered either giant tubs of chocolate ice cream with marshmallows or giant hot fudge sundaes. The Dairy was a big place with large booths, always crowded with teenage kids. There was a jukebox that played the big-band hits. And it was actually a dairy. If you went around the back, you could see the cows grazing.

"Annie was included in virtually all of my activities with The Cruiser, except for an occasional exploit of derring-do. I had a fascination with speed, and I used to rev up the convertible, which was hardly a fast vehicle, to maximum speed and 'shoot' the old B&O Railroad bridge. It was a risky endeavor because the bridge was only the width of one car and quite steep, which made it impossible for me to see oncoming traffic until I was over the crest. One day I was taking the bridge at top speed, on the fly, just as another car was coming from the other side. We would have collided if the driver hadn't slammed on his brakes at the last minute and swerved out of the way. I stopped the practice after that." ■

"Annie was included in virtually all of my activities with The Cruiser, except for an occasional exploit of derring-do."

TOM WOLFE
1953 Ford Country Squire Station Wagon

Tom Wolfe is a journalist and novelist. He is the author of many books, including The Right Stuff *and* The Bonfire of the Vanities. *Tom Wolfe was born and raised in Richmond, Virginia, and educated at Washington and Lee and Yale universities. In December 1956, he took a job as a reporter on the* Springfield (Massachusetts) Union. *This was the beginning of a 10-year newspaper career, most of it spent as a general assignment reporter. For six months in 1960 he served as The* Washington Post's *Latin American correspondent and won the Washington Newspaper Guild's foreign news prize for his coverage of Cuba. In 1970, he published two best-selling books on the same day.*

"I've only owned two cars in my life, although I love driving. I bought the first car in order to have a job on a newspaper—my first job. It was 1956, and I was a citywide reporter for the *Springfield Union* in Springfield, Massachusetts, and you had to have a car. So I bought a 1953 Ford Country Squire station wagon. Why, I don't know.

"It was one of the last station wagons that had wood on it. It had metal sides with big strips of wood. Today they do the same thing, but they make them out of fiberglass. It constantly grew mushrooms out of the wood. It would get wet, and I didn't have any place to put it. I had no garage or anything. It would get wet, and these mushrooms would grow and grow. It was a very strange car.

"I bought the car in '56. It was four years old when I bought it, and I kept it until 1962, when I came to New York. I took it to Washington and used it while I was working on the *Washington Post*. I used to park it on the street all the time. I always left the doors unlocked so that anybody who wanted to break in wouldn't have to break anything. However, a car with mushrooms growing out of it was not a prime target.

"I traveled a lot in it. It broke down once. I was traveling from Washington to Long Island for my summer vacation. It was 105 degrees that day, and the car broke down on the New Jersey Turnpike at Union City. I was so hot. I remember sitting by the side of the Turnpike. I don't know why, but I had a black umbrella, and I was eating cucumbers. I also don't know why I brought the cucumbers along, although I knew cucumbers had water in them, and it was really hot.

"They towed the car, with me in it, into Union City. And Union City, at least the part where they repaired cars, was the most woebegone, broken-down town you've ever seen in your life. They said it was going to take two or three hours to fix, so I started wandering around. And I came to understand the Catholic church in a way. There was, in the middle of this rotting section of town, an absolutely stunning stone cathedral. I knew that a stone building would be cool, so I went inside.

"The place was absolutely majestic. There were a few people inside lighting votive candles, going by the Stations of the Cross, and so on, and I thought to myself, 'Isn't it just great to have something like this, so that no matter what your circumstances—such as being homeless and adrift beside the Jersey Turnpike—you have this absolutely majestic place to go to that in some way is yours.' I was raised a Presbyterian, and Presbyterians don't build structures like that. It's against our religion actually.

"I used to park it on the street all the time. I always left the doors unlocked so that anybody who wanted to break in wouldn't have to break anything. However, a car with mushrooms growing out of it was not a prime target."

"I used to travel for 500 miles with $12 in my pocket because that was more than enough for gasoline."

"I think the Lord must have been watching, or I went to the right church perhaps, because they only charged me $35, and I had thought I was going to be taken and just depleted. However, it was the beginning of my vacation, and I had $35 with me. I used to travel for 500 miles with $12 in my pocket because that was more than enough for gasoline. When you're young, as long as you have three or four extra dollars for sandwiches—then you don't worry. It's great to feel that immune to things. I did love that car." ■

KEN GROSS
1948 Ford Club Coupe

Ken Gross is a well-known automotive author, journalist, and a noted expert on the history of hot rodding and customs. Gross is also an in-demand concours judge, and museum exhibit and automotive collection consultant. He is the former director of the Petersen Automotive Museum in Los Angeles.

"Hot rods and a hot rod attitude have always been important for me. I can't resist trying to make anything on wheels a little better. It's been that way since I bought my first issue of *Hot Rod* magazine, back in October 1954. One of my favorite high school memories is sitting in Miss Durgin's math class, staring out of the basement window straight into two big echo cans under the ribbed '37 DeSoto bumper on John Knowles' lowered, fender-skirted and primered '40 Ford coupe. I can close my eyes and still hear the hoarse cough of the flathead's starter, followed by the deep, intoxicating rumble of well broken-in steelpacks.

"That was 55 years ago, and it really gives you a perspective. Hot rodding started because guys wanted their cars to go faster and look cool. Hot rodders were still considered outlaws (we'd have said juvenile delinquents) when I was growing up in the balmy Eisenhower era, but things were changing. Henry Gregor Felsen's classic novel, *Hot Rod*, showed how tragedies could happen when youthful exuberance and the need for speed wasn't properly channeled. So Bud Coons and Eric Rickman criss-crossed the country in a red and white Plymouth station wagon, spreading the NHRA gospel to car-crazy kids, community leaders and cops, telling them that it was okay to soup up old cars, and that drag racing on sanctioned strips was the best youth management approach for every progressive community.

"It was a great era. Rock and roll was in its infancy; Chuck Berry sang about Maaaayyyybelline! Remember the line, 'Nuthin' outrunnin' my V-8 Ford?' Well, few stock models could. Guys would buy a used '40 Ford coupe for about $125. Dual exhausts, maybe with Fenton headers, if you had the scratch, were the first modification.

Here I am—crew cut, T-shirt, and all—parked in front of a neighbor's house in 1959. Big and littles, wide whites, that downhill stance, this '48 Ford Club Coupe had "the look," long before we called cars like these "resto-rods." Ken Gross collection

"But you didn't have to live in California. Pennsylvania's Ed Almquist, Chattanooga's Honest Charlie (or L.A.'s Lewie Shell, Roy Richter's Bell Auto Parts, or Chicago's Roy Warshawsky) would sell you a set of finned high-compression heads and a dual carb manifold for another $100 or so. Railway Express delivered them in those days. Add a hot cam for about $50, Lincoln-Zephyr valve springs and Johnson adjustable tappets, do a little porting and relieving and you were off to the (street or strip) races.

"More mechanically minded guys yanked big OHV V-8s out of wrecked Olds and Caddies. Most home-built cars were quicker ('til Chevy's high-revving, small-block V-8 arrived) than nearly anything you could get new. I bought a used '53 Olds V-8 engine from Harbor Auto Parts in Lynn, Massachusetts, for my '40 Ford coupe. It cost more than I paid for my coupe; it came out of a car that had been rear-ended. Honest Charlie supplied the adapter, a throw-out bearing, and a pair of front engine mounts. The big Olds was ready to drop right in, and then things changed, as I'll tell you later.

"I belonged to two Boston area hot rod clubs. First, I joined the Pipers of Swampscott, Massachusetts. Later I was a member of the Choppers of nearby Salem. One of our favorite haunts was Adventure Car Hop restaurant on Route 1 in Saugus. It was exactly one-quarter of a mile from the edge of the drive-in's parking lot to the first overpass on Route 1. Guys would choose off, idle out to the turnpike and stomp on it. You'd hear the screech of rubber, the whine of engines, and the shutoff, even over the loud music piped through carside speakers. The loser slunk home. The winner came back, idled around the parking lot in triumph, and ordered a Bermudaburger.

"I will never forget one summer night in Salem, standing in a gas station on Federal Street, and watching an older guy in the Choppers club, he might have been 22—I was in high school—rumble up in his chopped and lowered '49 Mercury. The car looked ominous, really sinister, as it rolled up the street, spinner hubcaps flashing. He had a DA haircut. Polite society called that rebel cut a ducktail—the initials stood for duck's ass—and only the tougher guys who took shop courses in school had 'em.

> "I belonged to two Boston area hot rod clubs. First, I joined the Pipers of Swampscott, Massachusetts. Later I was a member of the Choppers of nearby Salem."

"His Mercury had almost no visible chrome, no hood ornament, and no door or decklid handles. It was finished in blue oxide primer, which made it even more distinctive. And it was lower and sleeker than most contemporary cars on the street. Inside, his girlfriend snuggled close in the middle of the seat (we can thank bucket seats for eliminating that little benefit), the duals crackled with a guttural rumble that just added to this car's mystique. I wanted that Merc in the worst way, and probably so did every kid who saw it. I can close my eyes and still see and hear that car.

"My buddies and I all read the 'little books' like *Rod & Custom* and *Car Craft* in study hall. We stripped our cars of nonessential parts and unwanted chrome, dodged cops for loud muffler violations, and yes, before the Sanford, Maine, drag strip became an institution, we street raced.

Gross remains a committed enthusiast and hot rodder, still the owner of many flathead-powered Ford cars. Ken Gross collection

"I installed a set of 4-inch lowering blocks to get the rear down . . . so the car sat pretty low and rode like a truck. I didn't know anything about suspension travel and wouldn't have cared. I liked the way it looked."

"I was driving a '50 Chevy convertible that I bought in 1957 when I was 15, with $125 that I earned from delivering newspapers and mowing lawns. I dechromed it completely, filling all the holes, including the door handles, with fiberglass. The two-piece hood was bullnosed, I frenched the headlights with '52 Ford rims, and molded '52 Buick taillights horizontally in the panel below the decklid.

"John Sharrigan of the famous No-Mads Club in Allston, Massachusetts, louvered the hood. There were 90 louvers and I think they were a buck apiece. Slim's Auto Body in Lynn [Massachusetts] sprayed the car in black primer. We didn't know about adding flattener then, so if anyone touched the surface, they left prints. "Shag" also fabricated a dual exhaust system with both pipes exiting behind the driver's door. I'd run out of the money it would have taken for him to fabricate twin tailpipes.

"Along the way, I installed a set of 4-inch lowering blocks to get the rear down, and Eddie Vargabedian cut two coils out the front springs, so the car sat pretty low and rode like a truck. I didn't know anything about suspension travel and wouldn't have cared. I liked the way it looked.

"So did a kid named Tom Difocci from Lynn. He had a '40 Ford coupe project and had lost his storage. I wanted a "Fotty Foahd," as we'd have said with our Boston accents. No money changed hands; Tommy and I did a deal that saw me towing the unfinished '40 home. My parents thought I'd lost my mind. What self-respecting teenager would trade a running car (even, in their opinion, if he'd totally ruined its looks), for an engineless hulk?

"Of course, I had a plan. With my meager savings, I bought a rebuilt '39 Ford transmission, the installation kit, and the aforementioned Olds V-8. I didn't lack for knowledge; I read every hot rod mag there was, and several friends had done engine swaps. Paul Bourke had gone the Olds route with his '40, Phil Bernier stuffed an Olds into a '51 Chevy hardtop, and Eddie Belson installed a Plymouth V-8 in his '42 Ford business coupe. The '40 needed total rewiring; there were no instruments, and the seat was a tattered mess. The resurrection list was long and costly. Even more importantly, I really needed a car that ran.

"DiFocci came to the rescue again. Over at the Dairy Queen near Wyoma Square, he introduced me to a guy, I've forgotten his name, who had one of the cleanest '48 Ford Club Coupes [Ford officially called this model a Coupe Sedan]. It was black, and he'd installed '48 Merc 15-inch wheels, with 8.20 15 tires in back, 5.40 16s in front, and 6-inch front shackles for a little rake and a lot of unwanted side-sway. Even better, he came over to look at my '40 and offered to swap his car and threw in an additional $200. I jumped at it.

"My dad was a designer of women's sportswear and a real talent with a sewing machine. He stitched up a set of custom black Naugahyde seat covers with white piping that looked and fit really well. I changed out all the plastic dash panels for accessory chromed items. Dual exhausts with steelpack mufflers were a must. I couldn't afford headers, so I just removed the crossover pipe and capped the stock cast iron manifolds. I wanted a dual carb manifold and heads, but with college expenses looming, I decided I'd better save my money.

"This car was a resto-rod before that expression became popular. The little black coupe had 'the look,' even if, in the immortal words of *Mechanix Illustrated*'s jocular road tester, Tom McCahill, "it didn't have enough suds to pull a wet piece of gum out of a baby's mouth." Besides, I kept rationalizing that one of these days I'd just drop in a

Gross with his "ultimate Deuce Highboy." This car was completed only recently, after a multi-year, coast-to-coast search for the right combination of authentic 1932 Ford parts and period speed equipment to get just the right look without using any new or reproduction pieces.
Rebecca Kelly

big overhead. I never did. This probably explains why, because I was speed equipment–deprived as a kid, I have collected so many after-market Ford flathead intake manifolds today.

"My parents were afraid to let me take the car all the way up to St. Lawrence, the small college I attended, not far from the Canadian border, in upstate New York. They were certain I'd be distracted. They were right. I longed for my car, but I understood their concern. In the interim, my father commuted to Boston in my high school hot rod. Home on vacation, friends would ask, "Hey man, didja sell yuh cah? I saw an old guy driving it." I'd reply sheepishly, "That was my dad." Like me, he had prematurely gray hair. Finally, in my senior year, I was allowed to take my coupe to college.

"In those pre-Northway days, it was a solid nine-hour ride from Swampscott to Canton. Once I was back at school, I predicted a big change in my social life. That didn't happen. When I was in high school, girls thought my little coupe was cool. In college, I was competing against suave rich guys who drove Porsche 356s, Corvettes, Austin-Healeys, and Corvair Monzas. And it was so cold; without a plug-in block heater, the poor Ford often couldn't start. So much for a warm back seat for snuggling.

"In the frigid North Country, that anemic six-volt battery would grunt "err, err, errrrrrr," and nothing would happen. One snowy night, the car was actually running and I cautiously drove it, without snow tires, to pick up a girl at the dorm. The guy in front of me backed up right into the grille, crushing several bars. I'd removed the bumper guards for looks and my front end was lowered, remember?

"Luckily, a wrecking yard on the Potsdam-Canton Road had a black '48 Ford sedan. I took its grille out and swapped it for my damaged one. It was easy to find old Fords in junkyards 50 years ago. Try doing that today.

"That spring, with money tight and graduate school expenses looming, I knew I had to sell it. A fellow named Jeff Johns paid me $175 for the car, and he drove it to his home to Oklahoma. That sounds like a pathetic sum today, but it was a lot of money in 1963. I remember sadly watching him drive off in my coupe for the last time. And I still have a framed photograph of the Ford hanging in my office.

"I recently decided to try to find Mr. Johns. The college alumni office told me he last registered with them as living in Wycoff, New Jersey, and I also found his name listed in a golf tournament in the Garden State. Sadly, his phone number is unlisted. It's a slim chance Jeff still has that car, but perhaps he could tell me who he sold it to—and I can take up the search from there.

"I already have squirreled away a new set of Cyclone heads, a three-carb Cyclone intake, a Winfield SU-1A cam, and a freshly rebuilt Harman and Collins dual point/dual coil distributor all ready. A re-bore, bigger valves, adjustable tappets, a 4-inch Merc crank, and a 12-volt conversion would make a winner out of that 59AB engine. I'd be finishing a job I always wanted to do. A dropped axle would replace those long shackles. I've got just the right one hanging on the garage wall. I'm sure I could find a Columbia two-speed rear somewhere. And that's all—no cutting, no customizing."

EPILOGUE

"After agonizing for years about what happened to my old car, I wrote a story about it for *Old Cars Weekly* and included an email address. Almost immediately, six readers, led by Joe Miller in Middletown, Connecticut, sent emails with Jeff Johns' address and phone number.

"So I took a deep breath and made the fateful call.

"After convincing the lady who answered, a somewhat skeptical New Jersey type, that I meant no harm, 'Howdja get this number? It's unlisted,' followed by 'He's 67 years old. How's he gonna remember some old car he bought in college?' Jeff Johns called me back.

"'Hi Kenny,' he said, as though it hadn't been 46 years since we'd last talked at St. Lawrence, and I sadly watched as he drove my car away.

"Of course he remembered the coupe, and he seemed glad to talk about it. He'd owned the car for several years, installed a new flathead in it, and eventually sold it to his father, who in turn sold it to an uncle. Apparently the uncle 'drove it into the ground' and the car was junked.

"Jeff remembered my little coupe fondly, particularly the luscious black Naugahyde interior that my dad stitched up and installed.

"So there it is. After 46 years since I sold it, the end of the story. It's better to know what happened, I guess, and it's sad, but the little black coupe lives on forever, frozen in time, in a photo on my desk." ∎

> "It's better to know what happened, I guess, and it's sad, but the little black coupe lives on forever, frozen in time, in a photo on my desk."

Hugh Hefner

1941 CHEVY COUPE

These days, Mr. Hefner likely spends more time escorting Playboy Playmates in stretch limos than he would piloting his '41 Chevy, even if he still owned it. AP Photo/The Canadian Press/Chris Young

> ## *"I was still driving this car at the time, and the car finally quit in the middle of the street, the same day the magazine went on sale."*

Hugh Hefner is the founder of Playboy *magazine, and one of the major players of the modern the sexual revolution. Heffner stayed away from cliché media markets such as New York or Los Angeles, instead choosing to establish the Playboy empire in Chicago instead. Heffner must appreciate great automobiles, as cars are a staple editorial element of* Playboy, *and Heffner drove a relatively exotic Mercedes-Benz 300SL roadster in the 1960s.*

"My first car was a 1941 Chevy coupe that I bought in 1950. It cost about $400. It reminds me of the car Columbo used to drive. There's one experience I remember very well. I began *Playboy* in 1953. The first issue was undated, but it was actually a December issue that went on sale in November. I was still driving this car at the time, and the car finally quit in the middle of the street, the same day the magazine went on sale. I had a funny feeling when it happened. If the car could have talked, it would have said, 'You have to take it alone from here, pal.'" ∎

KEITH MARTIN
1959 Austin-Healey Bugeye Sprite

Keith Martin is founder of the Sports Car Market *magazine, books, and websites. Martin is a highly knowledgeable collector car market analyst, author, and consultant. He's owned a wide and eclectic variety of cars, and avidly supports their use and enjoyment.*

"At 8 a.m. on my 16th birthday, I was first in line at the local DMV, and successfully passed my test. I then went directly to a friend's house and bought his 1959 Austin-Healey bugeye Sprite for $30, which was a fair price, as it not only had no first or reverse gear, which created some challenges in hilly San Francisco, but the lower left front piece of the hood was simply missing, as if it had been bitten off by some metal-eating dinosaur.

"While my high school friends were busy cutting donuts in their new Oldsmobile 4-4-2s, I was bundling up at 6 in the morning to drive to places like Cotati and Laguna Seca Raceways to be an assistant corner worker for SCCA races. I saw marvelous things there, like bugeyes with tilt-forward front ends and carburetors with velocity stacks. I assume they all had first and reverse gears but I never asked.

"I rebuilt my car's engine with my stepfather's help, and overhauled the gearbox as well. Sadly, as I couldn't afford a new cluster gear, first and reverse soon became non-functional again, giving me the only three-speed Sprite in the Bay Area.

"My girlfriend went away to UC Santa Barbara, and my big adventure was driving the Sprite the 350 or so miles there and then back. I had peace and love symbols painted all over it, which might have something to do with why I was stopped every 50 or so miles by the California Highway Patrol for a "safety inspection." After the first one, I showed the succeeding officers my "rap sheet" of mechanical violations and they sent me on my way.

"My load-capacity record was five including driver, with two friends stuffed under the back deck behind the seats and two more in the cockpit—impressive, as the Sprite is a small, two-seat roadster. I could have used first gear that night as we went up the San Francisco hills.

Not a bugeye Sprite, but on of the many Alfa Romeos that Martin has owned. Keith Martin collection

"I don't remember who I sold it to, but I remember I got $250 for it, which was nearly enough to pay for the 'real car' that came next, a 1958 MGA convertible with a rod knock that I found in a junkyard. I tried to drive that one to the Chicago National Convention in 1968, with the side pockets in the doors filled with peace symbols to give to the chicks we were sure we would meet along the way, but that's another story." ∎

PETER EGAN
1959 Triumph TR-3

Peter Egan is one of America's foremost automotive storytellers; known best of his popular Side Glances column in Road & Track *magazine. Egan weaves stories that are as much about life as they are about cars, motorcycles, and the driving, riding, racing, and restoration of same. Compendiums of his columns have been assembled and published in book form.*

"The first car in my life was actually co-owned with my friend Ron Binter—a 1951 Buick that we tried unsuccessfully to turn into a stock car when we were 16.

"But the first real, *bona fide* car of my own, requiring license plates and ruinous insurance, was a 1959 Triumph TR-3, dark green in color, with a white top. I bought it for $450 in the spring of 1968, when I was a sophomore at the University of Wisconsin in Madison.

"My roommate, Pat Donnelly, and I had both been working nights, unloading trucks at the Coca-Cola bottling plant, and saving money for a pair of Triumph T100C motorcycles for a projected trip through Canada at the end of summer, but then we fell in love with two different [luckily] girlfriends and decided a couple of sports cars would be much swankier for dating purposes. Pat bought an MGA 1600 and I started looking for a TR-3.

"I found one in the Milwaukee *Journal* classifieds and, being normally on foot, took a Greyhound bus to Milwaukee to look at the car during our week of spring break. Pat went with me. The car had been recently repainted BRG [British Racing Green] and looked beautiful sitting in the parking lot of an apartment building. The Triumph belonged to a young seminary student who was about to become a Catholic priest. I thought perhaps he was giving up the things of thisworld, but it turned out he was mainly giving up driving.

"The TR-3 ran on just three of its four cylinders, so the owner knocked $100 off his $550 asking price and said he'd been told the car needed a valve job. At last; here was my golden opportunity to learn how to do a valve job. I paid the $450 and Pat and I went stuttering off on the 150-mile trip to my hometown. On the way home, I threw the car into a hard left sweeper in the Baraboo hills, and the lovely racing-type flip-up chromed gas cap flew off into the woods. We searched but never found it. That was the last hard corner I ever took without having a spoke punch through an innertube, causing a flat tire.

"When I got home, I did a compression check and found to my joy that the car needed not a valve job, but one new spark plug. Back to smooth running on all four.

"During spring break, I drove up to Wausau, Wisconsin, to visit my new girlfriend and future wife, Barbara. On that 100-mile trip, the car, sequentially, blew both radiator hoses, broke its fan belt, and got one flat tire. At the end of the weekend we drove back to college in

Peter Egan, circa his high school graduation.
Peter Egan collection

Egan's TR3 was the source of much adventure and frustration, and assuredly inspired some of his writings about the "joys" of old British sports cars. Peter Egan collection

"In short, the car almost drove me crazy—my first lesson in materialistic over-reaching and hubris."

a cold rainstorm and almost drowned—the top, side curtains, vents, door seams and windshield gasket all leaked and blew water on us and our belongings like so many NACA ducts, but Barb was not seriously fazed. A good omen.

"After that, I worked full time to pay for the car and repairs, but was always too broke to drive it much. I earned constant parking tickets for having it stationary for too long during curbside repairs, and on a dinner date to the Cole Hall spring formal I honked the horn and the whole wiring harness caught on fire and filled the car with black smoke. Barb and I—me in my best suit and she in a beautiful white dress and gloves—bailed out as the yellow dorm bus went by on its way to the spring formal, transporting all the poor saps who didn't have glamorous sports cars. We abandoned the car, I called a cab, and then I spent the next few days rewiring the car in a vacant lot along East Washington Avenue with rolls of hardware store bell wire. I encountered many grounding problems because the body was mostly a confection of Bondo and fiberglass mesh. Sort of like a homecoming float that looks like a TR-3, but is really made of roses. Or something more industrial and less fragrant.

"In short, the car almost drove me crazy—my first lesson in materialistic over-reaching and hubris. I'd angered the gods, and they were trying, as Allen Ginsberg would say, to make me a saint.

"I sold the car late in the summer to an older fellow in Milwaukee, who seemed undaunted by its many mechanical challenges, for $300. I bought a Honda CB160 motorcycle for $200 and took that on a 1,000-mile trip through Canada with Pat, on another Honda borrowed from my brother-in-law, and had no mechanical problems. Free at last.

"Loved the looks of the car, though. And the sound, and the torque, and the low doors. When I got home from Vietnam and out of the Army three years later, I bought another TR-3 the day before Barb and I got married. We towed it to our apartment with a Volkswagen Beetle and a piece of rope. But that's another story. A similar story, but a slightly different one." ∎

Carlton
is lowest.

Less than 1 mg.

230

Andy Warhol

1937 AND "1970-SOMETHING" ROLLS-ROYCE

Pittsburgh native and New York resident artist and filmmaker Andy Warhol was murdered in 1987 after many more than 15 minutes of fame. Warhol is credited as one of the founders of the modern "pop art" movement in the 1950s, his vivid graphics images of faces, or common popular objects such as the Coca Cola bottle, turning the art world on its collective ear. He was also an underground filmmaker of some note.

"I didn't get my first car when I was 16. I got it when I was 56. I got it last year, when I was learning to drive. Actually, I got two cars; one's a 1937 Rolls-Royce, the other's a 1970-something Rolls-Royce. They weren't expensive.

"My most memorable experience was when I was learning to drive and was out with my instructor, and I smashed into a taxi outside the Graybar Building in New York City. That was when I gave up on driving. I can't do two things at one time—like talk and chew gum. And I was trying to do two things at one time: drive and learn how to drive. No one was hurt, but I just got too nervous and gave up.

"So the cars are sitting up on blocks now in some garage here in town. I don't have time to go back and look at them, but I hang on to them. They're better than art." ■

> "My most memorable experience was when I was learning to drive and was out with my instructor, and I smashed into a taxi outside the Graybar Building in New York City."

Warhol had great cars but didn't drive them, more often taking a taxi. David McGough/DMI/Time Life Pictures/Getty Images

INDEX